LOS BARRIOS FAMILY COOKBOOK

Tex-Mex Recipes from the Heart of San Antonio

LOS BARRIOS FAMILY COOKBOOK

DIANA BARRIOS TREVIÑO

Foreword by Emeril Lagasse

Ⓥ VILLARD NEW YORK

Library of Congress Cataloguing-in-Publication Data

Treviño, Diana Barrios.
    Los Barrios family cookbook : Tex-Mex recipes from the heart of
  San Antonio / Diana Barrios Treviño.
        p.   cm.
ISBN 0-375-76097-0
1. Mexican American cookery.   I. Title.
TX715.2.S69 T74   2002   2002071347
641.5972—dc21

Villard Books website address: www.villard.com
Printed in the United States of America on acid-free paper

9 8 7

Book design by Barbara M. Bachman

To my father, the late José C. Barrios,

and my mother, Viola B. Barrios

A lifetime of love is what you have given me.

Eternal thanks is what I return.

FOREWORD

As the food correspondent for ABC's *Good Morning America*, I'm always looking for new tastes and cuisines in different regions of the country, especially those that involve local culture. We went in search of big Tex-Mex cooking, which San Antonio is known for. I chose Los Barrios from the many Tex-Mex restaurants in the city because I fell in love with Diana Barrios Treviño and the entire Barrios family. They've survived a rocky start and difficult times, all the while remaining true to their family business and the home-style Tex-Mex food they serve. The dishes they have created contain amazing combinations and flavors that many people don't get to experience. I wanted the rest of the country to sample what I was tasting. I wanted people to realize that true Tex-Mex cooking isn't just fajitas and burritos.

We did the segment from the Arneson River Theater on the Riverwalk. We were surrounded by mariachis and thousands of San Antonio fans. Diana brought platters and platters of enchiladas and tamales, and prepared a traditional Mexican dish that her mother makes, Pollo con Calabacita, a hearty home-style chicken dish with tatuma squash and oregano. After only a few minutes, my mouth began to water from the awesome aromas coming from the pot!

Later that day, I went by Los Barrios with my then girlfriend—now wife—Alden. What began as a late-afternoon lunch turned into a true feast. I managed to taste almost everything on the menu, which is no easy feat! The whole Barrios clan joined us at the table to help polish off the great food. The more food they brought, the more people showed up—our table just kept growing and growing. I felt right at home, because Los Barrios is all about family, and I now felt like a member of Diana's welcoming family.

Now, with the *Los Barrios Family Cookbook*, I am excited to know that people across the country can easily prepare and taste all of the delicious dishes I experienced on my visit. Whether you like your food hot, medium, or mild—and these recipes have it all—you'll love the food in this book. So go ahead, kick it up a notch San Antonio style!

EMERIL LAGASSE

gracias

ACKNOWLEDGMENTS

When Random House first approached Los Barrios in June of 1999 about doing a cookbook, my first reaction was one of excitement. But as I started to think about it, I began to get nervous. We weren't writers; we made enchiladas for a living. Yet throughout the entire process, we were blessed to work with a woman who had tremendous faith in us: Pamela Cannon, our editor, held my hand from beginning to end. During my pregnancy (and with the emotional roller coaster that came with it), through my broken ankle (she said it was a blessing because it would force me to sit still long enough to write this book), and all the way through our busy summers at the restaurant, Pamela was there. She gave me the confidence I needed to do this project and created a very special bond between us that will always be there. Thank you, Pamela, for your constant encouragement and for being such a great friend.

My father died in 1975, and it was a bad year for our family. The bright spot in that otherwise dark time was the arrival of Maria Marquez, who came to work with my mother. Maria has been with us through thick and thin, and is still very active on a day-to-day basis at Los Barrios. Her brother, José Luz Villegas, known as Lucio, has also been instrumental in our organization. I thank them both for their many years of support and loyalty. *Mil gracias por todo.*

Many thanks to everyone in my family for being so supportive. I thank my sister, Theresa, for putting up with my late-night phone calls to get her opinion on wording for a recipe and for letting me interrupt her even if she was with a patient. I thank my brother, Louie, for his great belief in me and in this project, and also for his collaboration in writing the story of our family. I would also like to thank my husband, Roland, and my sons, Jordan, Evan, and Diego. "Yes, boys, Mommy is done and we can play now."

And to my beautiful mother, Viola, thank you for teaching me everything you have taught me. If I can be a fraction of the woman you are, I will have succeeded.

CONTENTS

Foreword by Emeril Lagasse   *vii*

Acknowledgments   *ix*

Introduction   *xiii*

Stocking Your Kitchen   *xx*

Helpful Hints for Great Results Every Time   *xxi*

The "Must Haves"   1

Breakfast   15

Appetizers   29

Soups   57

Salads   75

Entrées   87

Side Dishes   149

Desserts   169

Beverages   187

Index   *197*

INTRODUCTION

In 1979, when my mother, Viola B. Barrios, invested $3,000 in an old garage to open her new restaurant, Los Barrios, she never imagined that it would someday be named one of the "100 Best New Restaurants in America" by *Esquire* magazine. Nor could she have pictured it eventually growing into a 280-seat restaurant packed with customers each and every day.

It seems that some things are special right from the very start. While $3,000 registers very little financially, Mama Viola's ambition and perseverance rank among the greatest ever.

Los Barrios did not begin as a dream but rather as a last hope. After the death of my father, debts started piling up and my mother was forced to take financial matters into her own hands. With two failed business ventures behind her, she turned to what she knew best. My mother had always been an incredible cook, keeping our tummies filled with the wonderful dishes that had been handed down to her through the generations. This wonderful home cooking is the true essence of Los Barrios.

Our beginnings were humble. We started in a $500-a-month garage that had previously been home to an outboard motor repair shop. This was all that we could afford at the time. There was no parking lot and there were no windows. The chairs and tables didn't match. A small metal front door serviced everyone from the fifty customers per day to the two employees, as well as the purveyors. At night, we just closed the garage door to lock up.

Mama Viola set high standards for her cuisine, knowing that when your ambience is humble, the food had better be *good*! And that's exactly what it was. My brother Louie's role was to run the "dining room," along with the help of one waiter, Juan. I was a junior in high school at the time and would visit during lunch whenever my girlfriends and I could sneak away from school.

Soon enough, everyone began to take notice of the little garage restaurant. First it was the downtown businesspeople, then the local food critics. One article referred to Francisco D. Rodríguez, who was my mother's original partner, affectionately known as

Paco, as "the Muhammad Ali of the restaurant industry" because of his quick wit. Before you knew it, the lines were out the door. With the lines also came challenges. The long hours in the restaurant business never allowed us much opportunity to revel in our success. The more customers we had, the more problems arose, and we needed to handle them.

Everyone helped out where they could, but it was Mama Viola who shouldered most of the burden. Not speaking English fluently did not seem to affect her progress. Of course, great cooking carries with it a lot of forgiveness.

The joys of the restaurant were plentiful, though. The relationships that were established, the memories that were created during times of great struggle, and the defining moments that made us who we were more than outweighed our troubles. I remember Paco dancing all by himself at the end of our first $500 day of sales. His solo salsa dance expressed joy, exhaustion, and relief. The relief carried with it a small sliver of the success that was to come. To this day, that moment of individual expression brings a tear of joy to my eyes.

When I think back to those early days, I often remember a couple named Mr. and Mrs. Rhett Butler (yes, really). We were in a business area of downtown San Antonio that would empty out after five o'clock. Most evenings, we had very few customers, and those few were the ones we got to know best. Rhett and his wife were two of them. I recall my mom and Paco making up dishes just for them. They were more like works of art than dinner. During those times, we also made our homemade sangría (see page 196), and, wow, was it delicious! The laughter of those days still lives in my memory. Today we still have a menu item named after Rhett, Nachos a la Butler (see page 51). I often joke that if the Butlers were ever to get a divorce, we would get custody of the nachos! Right from the start, Rhett was always pulling for our success, and although he lives in Paraguay today, he still sends us customers, to try the nachos named after him.

As the restaurant's popularity grew, so did the landlord's interest in our space—he tripled our rent after the first six months. That, along with Mama's dream to build a bigger restaurant, prompted us to make the move to our current location—4223 Blanco Road.

We made the move from downtown San Antonio into an old Dairy Queen on the near north side. It was built in the late 1950s and had a life of its own long before we came along. We've seen pictures of the young boys with their crew cuts, girls looking pretty in their poodle skirts, and, of course, the jukebox by the door. The Dairy Queen days are long gone, but we kept several mementos from that time. The original front-door frame is set in the middle of the dining room now, with the address numbers 4223 shining brightly above it. The brick walls that once held up the huge glass walls now support terra-cotta pots with luscious plants, adding life and color throughout the restaurant.

Although we were successful in our new space, we could seat only seventy-five people at one time, and that hardly produces enough revenue to make anybody wealthy. We've expanded three times, and we're now at full capacity with 280 seats. Still, however, the majority of our compensation comes in the form of gratitude from our customers when we are able to make their special occasions a little more special. And that, after all, is what fills up your emotional bank account. Considering the grief we had suffered over the loss of our father, it was just what the doctor ordered. All in all, it was part of the journey, part of the path set before us.

 FLYING SOLO

After four years in the business, Mama bought out Paco's interest in the restaurant. Paco wanted to be independent, which left Mama flying solo. She was not actually completely alone. You see, God had sent her a guardian angel, Maria Marquez, a young lady who has been my mother's right-hand person for almost all of her professional life. Together, the two women struggled, taking turns leaning on each other, and cooking all the way through.

With more than eight hundred Tex-Mex–style restaurants in San Antonio, to stand out here is to stand out in the land of the giants. One of the reasons Los Barrios does stand out is its cooking style and preparation. The *casero* style, which is a traditional Mexican home-cooking style, replicates recipes from those of our ancestors. For example, the recipe for Beef Stew Zuazua-Style (see page 90) came directly from Mama's godmother's kitchen in Zuazua, Nuevo León. The dish is composed of beef tenderloin cooked in a stew, with oregano for its strong flavor. Tortillas de Azúcar (Sugar Tortillas; see page 11) were prepared in our house on Sunday nights. I still remember the divine aroma that wafted from the kitchen and made its way throughout the house. It reminded us of Mama's motto, "Cooking for a loved one is a recipe for love." This expression is probably the main reason we decided to do a cookbook. It is a way of sharing our family's legacy with our friends.

Over these last twenty years, we have been a strong part of the San Antonio landscape. We have carved out a niche with the support of our many loyal customers and have been helped along the way by our friends in the media and the culinary arts. Through their assistance, we have had the privilege of helping out many charities and causes. In Spanish, there is the saying *Una mano lava la otra y juntas se lavan la cara* (One hand washes the other and together they wash the face). These acts of giving back to the community have brought us new friends and many good times.

I've often said that one of the most important things a family can do is to invite someone into their home for dinner. It is a way to share a little of oneself in this busy world. Unfortunately, the restaurant lifestyle does not allow us the freedom to do much of that type of entertaining. However, we are always willing to give of ourselves to both familiar customers and total strangers. In return, our lives resonate with love and gratitude.

Growing up in the restaurant business changes the way you view chores and work. We all find ourselves in the middle of so many celebrations—seeing our friends when they are at leisure and having fun—that it really never feels like work. I remember when the singing star Selena came into the restaurant at closing time with her band and her family. We, of course, agreed to stay open late and accommodate the hungry group. The way they acted was so special—they seemed as if they were on vacation together. Their relationships seemed precious, joking and kidding around with everyone, including us. The next day, Selena and her publicist, Robert Treviño, proceeded to play a joke on me by calling twice and saying that Selena had gotten sick from our food. One call came in the middle of our lunch rush, when the place was in its full glory; the second was two hours later. Robert pretended that Selena was unable to perform because of her illness and that Abraham, her father, was boiling mad. The two thoroughly enjoyed listening to me sweat during our conversations. Finally, they let me in on their joke as they laughed uncontrollably, until I, too, joined in. That memory of Selena and our restaurant is one that I will always cherish. It was déjà vu when I saw the scene re-created in the 1997 movie about her life.

In the restaurant business, things do not always go as planned. You constantly shoot from the hip and hope for the best. The fast-paced nature of the business has a way of always keeping us ready for the unexpected—such as the time "the bankers and the lawyers," as we like to call them, reserved the whole restaurant for after their softball game. After dinner, they were having so much fun that one person slung a tortilla to another as if it were a Frisbee. Before you knew it, a hundred tortillas were flying through the air—it looked as if a Mexican UFO invasion were taking place!

 ## OUR MISSION

Los Barrios has become the kind of place where families grow up. We watch as a family of two becomes a family of four, a son becomes a movie director, a daughter becomes a judge. The births, graduations, and other milestones in people's lives that have been celebrated at our restaurant have been a part of our family's life as well.

At Los Barrios, our mission is to be a part of your family, large or small. Sooner or later, people come home to visit their roots. An elderly customer was in a nursing home, and when her nurse asked if she wanted anything, she would answer, "A Number 2 and a margarita" (see page 191). Her daughter would say, "Mama, we're not at Los Barrios." "I know that," the woman would retort, "but she keeps asking me what I want, and I want a Number 2 and a margarita." When she passed on, her wake was held at Los Barrios, and each member of the family ordered a Number 2 and a margarita.

When my mother first set out, she struggled not only to build a business, but also to raise a family. She made many sacrifices, and the decisions she made turned out to be the right ones. Today, she has eight grandchildren ranging from fourteen months to twelve years of age. The older ones help out where they can. They have been known to seat people, make Limonada Fresca (see page 190), roll up the silverware, make tortillas, work the cash register, and even tell a joke or two at a table. It's the family way.

My brother, Louie, was given the 1995 Small Business Leader of the Year Award by the Greater San Antonio Chamber of Commerce and was the recipient of the 1996 Restaurateur of the Year Award from the San Antonio Restaurant Association. My sister, Teresa, now a prominent podiatrist in San Antonio, also worked alongside us during her summer breaks and whenever school wasn't in session. Los Barrios has also had its share of distinctions. Along with recognition by *Esquire* magazine and features in *The*

New York Times, Los Barrios has been ranked one of the "Fifty Best Hispanic Restaurants" by *Hispanic* magazine.

I have been fortunate enough to represent San Antonio and Los Barrios on ABC's *Good Morning America* with Emeril Lagasse and on *Food Nation with Bobby Flay* on the Food Network. Although these have been very special moments for me and for my family, the following letter, written by a customer, expresses in words the emotions we at Los Barrios would like all of our customers to experience.

March 10, 1988

Dear Mrs. Viola Barrios,

Thank you for the fine lunch my friend and I enjoyed at your restaurant and thank you for your positive comments about the story I wrote.

I was born and grew up in Fort Worth. My father died when I was nineteen years old, nearly twenty years ago. His love for Mexico was something I will always remember. He made a number of trips to the interior to hunt and fish and visit friends. Because he was sixty-three years old when I was born, I didn't get to go with him on his frequent trips, but we did make it to Monterrey one time. I quickly sensed what was special about that country for him.

I moved to Eagle Pass twelve years ago and my daughter was born there. Although I felt alien to that town, there were times in Piedras when I knew if my father were alive, we would both feel welcome. It is a sadness and loss to me that he was not alive to cross with me and my daughter to Mexico.

That feeling of loss disappeared when I moved to San Antonio. The only time I have felt it since was the first time or two I visited Los Barrios. Your restaurant recalled for me all the good things that my father told me about his times in Mexico. Los Barrios just has that "feel," that quality of what is purely Mexicana and what was purely fine in his *compadres*.

Again, thank you for allowing me to do the story on your restaurant. And thank you for creating a place away from my hometown where I can find bittersweet memories of my father.

Sincerely,
Deborah Harding

Finally, I just want to say that cooking is a learned process: The more you practice, the better you get. It is an expression of your love for someone. Even if it doesn't taste wonderful, it still says "I love you." And there is nothing wrong with that. So I want to invite you to take the dive into your kitchen and start expressing yourself. Who knows, maybe someday that work of art will have been prepared by you!

Buen provecho from our family table to yours!

If you are lucky enough to be in the San Antonio area, we would love for you to stop by the restaurant. Please visit us at:

LOS BARRIOS RESTAURANT
4223 BLANCO ROAD
SAN ANTONIO, TX 78212

If you can't get to San Antonio to sample our wonderful food, you can still taste the restaurant dishes at home. The recipes in this book that we serve at Los Barrios are indicated by ☀ .

STOCKING YOUR KITCHEN

Mexican cooking is very simple and very basic. You can use a lot of the same ingredients and do different things with them. Stock your kitchen with the items listed below, and you'll be able to experience a whole new world of fast and easy cooking.

A COMBINATION OF SALT, PEPPER, AND GARLIC POWDER: Keep this in a shaker and use it to season everything; use twice as much salt as pepper and garlic powder. My mother gave me this tip the day I married.

TOMATOES, ONIONS, GARLIC, AND BELL PEPPERS: We use these in many recipes.

SERRANO, JALAPEÑO, AND ANCHO *CHILES*: We keep *chiles* with all degrees of heat on hand to satisfy everyone's palate, or mood!

CORN AND FLOUR TORTILLAS: These are essential. We eat these with everything (and on their own, with nothing else).

FLOUR, CORN *MASA* MIX, SALT, AND SHORTENING: You never know when you'll want to make fresh flour or corn tortillas.

AVOCADOS: My cousin calls these Mexican butter. The pebbly-skinned dark Hass avocados are our favorite.

FRYER CHICKENS: Keep one in the freezer for emergencies. You'll find many recipes you can prepare with them that will knock your family's socks off.

***QUESO CHIHUAHUA* AND MONTEREY JACK:** These can be used interchangeably in all of our recipes.

HELPFUL HINTS FOR GREAT RESULTS EVERY TIME

- Onions and garlic will keep for up to one month in the pantry or another cool, dark place.

- Keep vegetable oil in a cool, dark place and use within six months of purchase.

- Because nuts can turn rancid quickly, it's best to store them, in a tightly sealed container, in the freezer, where they will keep for up to six months.

- Keep spices in tightly sealed containers to preserve their flavor. Replace spices after one year.

- Organization is important in cooking—have all your ingredients prepared and lined up on the counter, or near the stove, in the order you will be using them.

- Most of the recipes in this book can be doubled, for larger groups.

- Use a *molcajete*—the Mexican version—or another type of mortar and pestle to grind herbs, spices, and other flavorings such as garlic, for better flavor.

- Heavy pots and pans are best, especially for long-cooked dishes.

- For the best flavor and texture, quick-cook vegetables in boiling salted water for 1 to 2 minutes only, until crisp-tender.

- When cooking skinless, boneless chicken breasts, brush them with olive oil before pan-frying, baking, or grilling; this will help keep them moist.

- For most recipes, cream cheese, sour cream, and eggs should be at room temperature. (For safety's sake, though, do not let the eggs sit out for more than 20 to 30 minutes before using them.)

- Heat store-bought tortillas in the microwave for just a few seconds before serving.

- For medicinal purposes, always keep a bottle of tequila on hand.

- For a great theme party, give a tequila tasting, with several different types and brands. Remember, sip, don't chug!

THE "MUST HAVES"

Enchilada Gravy Sauce   3

Homemade Corn Tortillas   4

Homemade Flour Tortillas   6

Los Barrios Salsa   7

Make-Me-Crazy Grill Marinade   8

Pico de Gallo   9

Salsa Ranchera   10

Sugar Tortillas   11

Tortilla Chips   12

Warm Mild Tomato Sauce   13

ENCHILADA GRAVY SAUCE

Makes 3 quarts

1 cup vegetable oil

2 cups all-purpose flour

¼ cup chili powder

1 tablespoon ground cumin

1 tablespoon garlic powder

1½ tablespoons salt

¼ teaspoon pepper

2 quarts water

1. Heat the oil in a large heavy saucepan over medium heat. Add the flour and cook, stirring constantly, until the flour is browned (this mixture is called a roux); be careful not to let the flour burn. Stir in the chili powder, cumin, garlic powder, salt, and pepper and cook, stirring constantly, for 2 to 3 minutes.

2. Gradually add the water, stirring until smooth. Cook, stirring frequently, for 5 minutes, then reduce the heat and boil gently for 15 minutes.

Use this sauce for enchiladas stuffed with cheese, beef, or chicken. Top them off with Chili con Carne (see page 115) and grated cheese. You can assemble them ahead of time and freeze them for future use. To serve, thaw them in the refrigerator, then heat in a conventional oven or the microwave.

Corn and flour tortillas (see page 6) are a staple in our home. They are eaten with every meal and used in many different recipes. The tortilla is to San Antonio as the bagel is to New York. It is the third utensil: the knife, the fork, and the tortilla! Serve these with butter, and use them to mop up the flavorful sauces on your plate.

Makes eight 4-inch tortillas

> 2 cups corn *masa* mix (see Note)
> 1½ cups warm water

1. Combine the *masa* mix and warm water in a medium bowl, mixing until a soft dough forms. You can use a wooden spoon for mixing, but you will have better results if you use your hands. Turn the dough out onto a floured surface and knead until it is smooth. If the dough seems dry, add more water, a tablespoon at a time, as necessary.

2. To form the tortillas, one at a time, pinch off small handfuls (about 3 tablespoons) of the dough and roll each one between the palms of your hands into a ball. Cover the dough balls with a damp cloth as you form them, to keep them from drying out.

3. Cut a quart-size resealable plastic bag open down both sides, to form a rectangle. Use the bag to line a tortilla press as you shape the tortillas, so they do not stick: Lay one side of the plastic over the bottom of the press, place a ball of dough in the center, and fold the other side of the plastic over the dough. Shut the top of the tortilla press firmly down on the dough to shape the tortilla. (See Note.)

4. Heat a griddle until hot. Place a tortilla on the griddle and cook for 1½ minutes. Using a spatula, flip it over and continue to cook, flipping it occasionally, until both sides are covered with small brown spots. Transfer to a plate and cover with a kitchen towel to keep warm while you cook the remaining tortillas, stacking the finished tortillas on the plate. Serve immediately.

NOTE: If you can't get your hands on a tortilla press, a clean countertop will do. You will still need the plastic so that the dough does not stick to the counter. Place a dough ball on one side of the plastic, cover with the other side, and use a heavy skillet to press out the tortilla.

Masa mix can be found at Latin markets and some larger supermarkets.

HOMEMADE FLOUR TORTILLAS

Making tortillas from scratch can be a lot of fun, but it can also be a little frustrating. My eleven-year-old son, Jordan, rolls his tortillas out into perfect circles, but mine end up looking like the state of Texas! Don't give up if they don't come out right on the first try. Once you get the hang of them, everyone will be asking for more. These will keep, well wrapped, for up to 1 week in the refrigerator and up to 2 months in the freezer.

Makes sixteen 6-inch tortillas

2½ cups all-purpose flour
1 teaspoon salt
½ teaspoon baking powder
⅓ cup vegetable shortening
⅓ cup hot water, or as necessary

1. Combine the flour, salt, and baking powder in a large bowl. Add the shortening and hot water, mixing until a soft dough forms.

2. Divide the dough into 16 pieces and shape each into a ball (these are called *testales*). On a floured surface, using a floured rolling pin, roll out each ball to a 6-inch circle.

3. Heat a griddle until hot. Place a tortilla on the griddle and cook until the bottom is lightly browned in spots, 1 to 2 minutes; the tortilla will puff up. Turn and cook until lightly browned in spots on the second side. Place in a towel-lined basket and cover with the towel to keep warm while you cook the remaining tortillas. Serve immediately.

VARIATION: For extra flavor and crunch, add 1 cup finely chopped pecans to the dough, mixing thoroughly.

LOS BARRIOS SALSA

This salsa is great with Tortilla Chips (see page 12). The only problem is that it quickly becomes habit-forming—you just can't stop eating it. We serve a bowl of this salsa and a basket of warm tortilla chips to every table in our restaurant, and people always ask for more. I have even seen customers eating it with a spoon, like soup. It goes with everything, from breakfast to dinner, and it accompanies every meal at Los Barrios. It will keep for up to 4 days in the refrigerator and can be frozen for up to 2 months.

Makes 4 cups

One 16-ounce can whole tomatoes
One 4-ounce can jalapeño *chiles*
1 teaspoon garlic powder
½ teaspoon salt
⅛ teaspoon pepper

Combine the tomatoes, *chiles,* garlic powder, salt, and pepper in a blender and blend to a chunky puree; do not blend until smooth. Transfer to a serving bowl.

VARIATION: You can make this hotter by increasing the amount of *chiles.*

Stir this salsa into individual servings of soup, or use it to top Shrimp Quesadillas (see page 136) or as an accompaniment to fajitas.

MAKE-ME-CRAZY GRILL MARINADE

This is a great marinade for chicken fajitas, fish, or shrimp. I seal everything in a Ziploc bag, place it in the refrigerator, and marinate for 2 to 4 hours, to ensure that the flavor soaks in. Remove from the refrigerator 30 minutes to 1 hour before grilling.

Makes 1½ cups

⅓ cup lime juice

⅓ cup lemon juice

⅓ cup orange juice

1½ tablespoons minced garlic

1 teaspoon dried oregano

¾ teaspoon ground cumin

1 bay leaf

Salt and pepper to taste

½ cup Los Barrios Salsa (see page 7) or your favorite store-bought brand

2 tablespoons olive oil

Combine all the ingredients in a blender and blend well.

PICO DE GALLO ✺

Serve this on the side with chicken or beef fajitas or as a dip for Tortilla Chips (see page 12). We have some customers who like to combine *pico de gallo* with our delicious Chile con Queso (see page 40) or add it to Charro-Style Beans (see page 151) for extra flavor.

Makes 3 cups

> 3 ripe tomatoes, diced
>
> 1 onion, diced
>
> 2 to 4 serrano *chiles* (to taste), thinly sliced
>
> ½ cup chopped cilantro
>
> Juice of 1 lime
>
> Salt and pepper to taste

Combine all the ingredients in a bowl and mix well.

VARIATION: Add ½ cup finely diced mango and ½ cup chopped jicama for a little flair.

SALSA RANCHERA

This salsa keeps well in the refrigerator for up to 1 week. Reheat gently before serving.

Makes 6 cups

6 tomatoes

4 cups water

5 serrano *chiles,* cut into thin strips

½ onion, quartered and thinly sliced

¼ cup vegetable oil

¼ teaspoon garlic powder

½ teaspoon salt

⅛ teaspoon pepper

1. Put the tomatoes in a large saucepan, add the water, and bring to a boil. Cook until the skins start to split, 10 to 12 minutes. With a slotted spoon, remove the tomatoes from the water; set the pan aside.

2. Peel the tomatoes and return them to the pan of water. Using a potato masher, thoroughly mash the tomatoes, blending them with the water. Add the *chiles,* onion, and oil and bring to a simmer over low heat. Simmer for 20 minutes, or until slightly thickened. Season with the garlic powder, salt, and pepper, and serve hot.

Use this spicy salsa to accompany steaks and other meat dishes, or top sunny-side-up eggs with it to make huevos rancheros. Or just serve with Tortilla Chips (see page 12) for a great snack.

SUGAR TORTILLAS

Tortillas de Azúcar

As I mentioned in the Introduction, this recipe is nearest and dearest to my family's heart. It was as much of a treat for my sister, brother, and me when we were growing up as it is for our children now. My son Evan loves to ask my mom for *tortillas* "*choquitas.*" What he means is *tortillas chiquitas,* little tortillas. Try these, and begin making your own memories.

Makes twenty-four 3-inch tortillas

> 4 cups all-purpose flour
>
> 1 cup sugar
>
> 1 teaspoon baking soda
>
> 1 cup vegetable shortening
>
> 2 eggs
>
> ¼ cup milk

1. Combine the flour, sugar, and baking soda in a large bowl. Add the shortening, blending well. Beat the eggs and milk together in a small bowl, then add to the shortening mixture, mixing well.

2. Turn the dough out onto a floured surface and knead until smooth. With floured hands, divide the dough into 24 pieces and roll into balls about the size of a golf ball. Using a floured rolling pin, roll each ball out into a round about 3 inches wide and ¼ inch thick.

3. Heat a griddle until hot. Place 2 or 3 tortillas on the griddle and cook until the bottoms are lightly browned in spots, 1 to 2 minutes. Turn and cook until lightly browned in spots on the second side. Place in a towel-lined basket and cover with the towel to keep warm while you cook the remaining tortillas. Serve immediately, with butter.

Store these in an airtight container. If they start to taste stale, reheat them on a cookie sheet in a preheated 350°F oven for 1 to 2 minutes. Watch carefully, since they can burn easily.

Makes about 11 dozen chips

2 cups vegetable oil

32 corn tortillas, homemade (see page 4) or store-bought,

    cut into quarters

Salt to taste

---

1.   Heat the oil in a deep heavy pot over medium-high heat until hot. Working in small batches, carefully drop the tortillas into the hot oil; be careful not to crowd the pot. Cook until crisp, 3 to 5 minutes (to check, remove a chip from the oil with a slotted spoon, let cool slightly, and taste it; if it is still a little chewy, the chips need to cook slightly longer).

---

2.   Using a slotted spoon, transfer to paper towels to drain briefly, then season lightly with salt.

VARIATION: As an alternative to the deep-fried chips, steam quartered corn tortillas until hot and serve them with salsa or dip.

Tortilla chips, or tostadas, as we call them, can be used in many different ways. They are great, of course, for dipping in salsa (see pages 7 and 10) or Guacamole (see page 47). They make the perfect base for a big plate of nachos (see pages 51 and 53). Or you can just nibble them on their own.

WARM MILD TOMATO SAUCE

Salsa Dulce de Tomate

Not everyone can handle the super-hot, spicy salsas available in the market today. Well, not to worry. This one's nice and mild.

Makes 1 to 2 cups

4 tomatoes, quartered

¼ cup vegetable oil

1 onion, thinly sliced

½ green bell pepper, thinly sliced

¼ teaspoon garlic powder

⅛ teaspoon ground cumin

½ teaspoon salt

¼ teaspoon pepper

1. Put the tomatoes in a blender and blend until pureed. Set aside.

2. Heat the oil in a medium skillet over medium heat. Add the onion and bell pepper and cook until soft, 3 to 5 minutes. Add the pureed tomatoes, garlic powder, cumin, salt, and pepper and bring to a simmer. Reduce the heat and simmer gently for about 45 minutes. Serve warm.

NOTE: If the tomatoes aren't very red, you can add a little canned tomato sauce to the pan.

BREAKFAST

Breakfast Chilaquiles 17

Hearty Fruit-and-Nut Oatmeal 18

Mama's Breakfast 19

Mexican Sausage and Eggs 20

Mexican-Style Eggs 21

Nature's Breakfast 22

Potato and Egg Tacos 23

Potato Tacos with Ancho Chile Sauce 24

Sassy Biscuits 26

Spicy Hash Browns 27

BREAKFAST CHILAQUILES

If you are going to cheat on a diet, this is the plate for you. The tostadas (tortilla chips) give these the Frito pie (corn chips in chili) crunchy effect. But remember, just don't cheat too often!

Serves 1 or 2

2 tablespoons vegetable oil

¼ cup diced onion

½ cup crushed tortilla chips (no smaller than ½ inch in size), homemade (see page 12) or store-bought

2 eggs, beaten

½ cup shredded American or Velveeta cheese

½ cup Salsa Ranchera (see page 10) or prepared tomato sauce

1. Heat the oil in a medium skillet over medium heat. Add the onion and tortilla chips and cook, stirring, until the onion is softened, 2 to 3 minutes. Add the eggs and scramble them with the onion and tortilla chips, 2 to 3 minutes.

2. Transfer the eggs to a plate (or plates) and top with the cheese and sauce.

Serve these with Refried Beans (see page 163) and warm flour tortillas (see page 6). This is a great way to begin Sunday morning.

HEARTY FRUIT-AND-NUT OATMEAL

Need a great breakfast to get you through a crazy day? Try this oatmeal, and get ready to conquer the world!

Serves 2

> Two 1.5-ounce packages instant oatmeal
> 1 cup milk
> 1 banana, sliced
> ½ cup dried cranberries
> ½ cup granola
> ½ cup chopped pecans or walnuts

1. Prepare the oatmeal according to package directions, substituting the milk for water.

2. Divide the banana, cranberries, granola, and pecans between 2 cereal bowls. Spoon the oatmeal over the fruit and nuts.

MAMA'S BREAKFAST

When my family and I had to move in with my mother because our house sold so quickly, she spoiled us by making this breakfast almost every day. It was really hard to leave her house, not only because we knew we would miss her, but also because we would miss this great breakfast. (If you want to serve more than two, make the breakfast in individual batches rather than doubling or tripling the recipe.) What a great way to start the day. Happy Breakfast!

Serves 1 or 2

2 tablespoons vegetable oil

2 tablespoons chopped onion

½ to 1 serrano *chile* (to taste), finely chopped

2 tomatoes, halved and grated on the large holes of a box grater

2 eggs, beaten

Salt to taste

1. Heat 1 tablespoon of the oil in a small skillet over medium heat. Add the onion and *chile* and cook until the onion is softened, 3 to 4 minutes. Add the tomatoes and simmer for 3 to 5 minutes (if the mixture looks dry, stir in a bit of water). Remove from the heat.

2. Heat the remaining 1 tablespoon oil in a medium skillet over medium heat. Add the eggs and scramble them for just 2 minutes; they should still be runny. Stir in the tomato mixture and season with salt.

Serve this with Refried Beans (see page 163), Hot Fried Potatoes (see page 156), and warm flour tortillas (see page 6), bolillos (small, elongated hard rolls), or 6-inch French breads.

MEXICAN SAUSAGE AND EGGS

Chorizo con Huevos

Serves 4

¾ pound chorizo (Mexican sausage), casings removed

4 eggs, beaten

Salt to taste

8 flour tortillas, homemade (see page 6) or store-bought

1. Sauté the sausage in a large skillet for 3 to 4 minutes. Drain the fat from the pan, add the eggs, and season with salt. Scramble the eggs with the sausage, 2 to 3 minutes.

2. Spoon the sausage mixture onto one side of each tortilla, dividing it evenly. Fold the tortillas over, and place 2 on each plate.

This dish goes well with Refried Beans (see page 163) and can be enjoyed as a midnight snack, as well as at breakfast.

MEXICAN-STYLE EGGS ☀

Huevos a la Mexicana

My father loved breakfast. When my mother made him this dish, he would moan with delight as he ate it. She would always ask him not to make so much noise, but his heart could not contain itself.

Serves 6

> 1 tablespoon vegetable oil
> ½ cup diced onion
> 3 to 4 serrano *chiles* (to taste), thinly sliced
> 2 tomatoes, diced
> 12 eggs, beaten

1. Heat the oil in a large skillet over medium heat. Add the onion and *chiles* and sauté until the onions are softened, 2 to 3 minutes. Add the tomatoes and cook for 3 to 4 minutes.

2. Add the eggs and scramble them with the other ingredients; do not overcook the eggs— they should still be a bit loose.

Serve with a side of Refried Beans (see page 163) and warm flour tortillas (see page 6).

NATURE'S BREAKFAST

Serves 6

1 cup strawberries, washed, hulled, and quartered

2 bananas, cut into ½-inch slices

½ cup dried cranberries

2 cups uncooked old-fashioned or quick-cooking oatmeal

1 cup granola

3 cups plain or flavored yogurt

½ cup chopped pecans

2 tablespoons honey

1. Layer the fruit in the bottom of 6 cereal bowls, dividing it evenly. Sprinkle the oatmeal and the granola over the fruit.

2. Top with the yogurt, and then the pecans and honey.

POTATO AND EGG TACOS

Tacos de Papa con Huevos

Makes 8 tacos

> ½ cup vegetable oil
> 1 potato, peeled and cut into ¼-inch dice
> 6 eggs, beaten
> Salt and pepper to taste
> 8 flour tortillas, homemade (see page 6) or
> store-bought, warmed

1. Heat the oil in a large skillet over medium heat. Add the potato and cook, stirring occasionally, until golden brown, about 5 minutes.

2. Pour off all but 1 tablespoon of the oil from the pan and add the eggs. Season with salt and pepper and scramble the eggs for 2 to 3 minutes.

3. Scoop the eggs onto one side of each tortilla, dividing them evenly. Fold over, and enjoy.

The eggs can be served without the tortillas as a main dish, along with Refried Beans (see page 163), or as a side to Breakfast Chilaquiles (see page 17). You could also serve them with toasted sliced French bread.

POTATO TACOS WITH ANCHO CHILE SAUCE

Tacos de Papa con Chile Colorado

These tacos are so good that you just keep on eating them, not realizing how many you've had! They are great to make when you have a cup or two of leftover mashed potatoes. My mother taught us never to throw anything away—you can always prepare something with leftovers.

Makes 8 tacos

2 potatoes, peeled and quartered

½ teaspoon salt, plus more to taste

¼ cup evaporated milk

2 tablespoons butter, at room temperature

White pepper to taste

1 ancho *chile*

½ cup water

1 tablespoon vegetable oil, plus more for frying

8 corn tortillas, homemade (see page 4) or store-bought

1. Put the potatoes in a large pot and add water to cover by 2 to 3 inches. Add the ½ teaspoon salt and bring to a boil. Cook until the potatoes are tender, about 15 minutes.

2. Drain the potatoes and return them to the pot. Add the evaporated milk and the butter, and season with salt and white pepper. Using a handheld mixer, beat until light and fluffy. Set aside.

3. Cut the *chile* in half and remove and discard the seeds and stem. Put the *chile* in a small saucepan, add water to cover by 2 inches, and bring to a boil. Cook for 5 minutes; drain and let cool. Remove the loosened skin from the *chile,* and put the halves in a blender. Add the ½ cup water, season with salt, and blend for 30 seconds to a puree.

4. Heat the 1 tablespoon oil in a small skillet over medium-high heat. Add the *chile* puree, reduce the heat to low, and cook for 5 minutes. Remove from the heat.

5. Pour 1 inch of oil into a large deep skillet and heat over medium-high heat until very hot. Using tongs, dip the tortillas one at a time in the hot oil for 5 to 10 seconds. Transfer to paper towels to drain.

6. Spread some *chile* puree over the tortillas. Spoon some potato mixture to one side of each tortilla, dividing it evenly among all of them, then fold the other half of the tortilla over the potato mixture. Brush the remaining puree over the outsides of the tortillas.

7. Heat a griddle or large skillet over medium heat until hot. Working in batches, place the tacos on the griddle and cook, turning once, until crispy, 1 to 2 minutes on each side. Serve immediately.

SASSY BISCUITS

Biscuits will never be the same once you try these. Sassy Biscuits are traditional in our home on Christmas morning. We make a nonspicy version first, for the children, then add jalapeño *chiles* to the dough for the adults. Delicious!

Makes 12 to 14 biscuits

1½ cups buttermilk biscuit mix

¼ cup cooked chopped chorizo (Mexican sausage)

½ green bell pepper, diced

½ red bell pepper, diced

2 scallions, sliced

½ cup shredded Cheddar cheese

½ cup buttermilk

1. Preheat the oven to 350°F. Lightly grease a baking sheet.

2. Combine the biscuit mix, sausage, peppers, scallions, and cheese in a large bowl. Add the buttermilk and stir until a soft dough forms. Turn the dough out onto a lightly floured surface and gently knead just until it comes together.

3. Using a floured rolling pin, roll the dough out to a ¾-inch thickness. Using a floured 2-inch biscuit cutter, cut out the biscuits and place them on the prepared baking sheet.

4. Bake for 12 to 14 minutes, until golden brown. Serve hot.

Serve these biscuits with scrambled eggs and your favorite salsa (see pages 7 and 10), or enjoy them on their own with butter.

SPICY HASH BROWNS

Papas Rancheras

These are a great Mexican twist on classic American hash browns.

Serves 6

½ cup vegetable oil

4 potatoes, peeled and cut into ¼-inch-thick slices

½ cup chopped onion

¾ cup diced tomatoes

2 to 3 serrano *chiles* (to taste), thinly sliced

1½ cups shredded *queso Chihuahua* or Monterey Jack cheese

1. Heat the oil in a large skillet over medium heat. Add the potatoes and cook, stirring occasionally, until tender, 4 to 5 minutes. Using a slotted spoon, transfer the potatoes to paper towels to drain for 5 minutes.

2. Pour off all but 1 tablespoon of the oil from the skillet. Set the skillet over medium heat and add the cooked potatoes, onion, tomatoes, and *chiles.* Cook until the onion is softened, about 3 minutes. Scatter the cheese over the potatoes, remove from the heat, and let stand until the cheese melts.

Serve these with eggs or Refried Beans (see page 163), or wrap them up in flour tortillas (see page 6) to make burritos.

APPETIZERS

Acapulco-Style Ceviche   31

Avocado Cocktail   33

Avocado Mini Tapas   34

Beachfront Veggies   35

Beef or Chicken Empanadas   36

Ceviche Cocktail   38

Chicharrón de Queso   39

Chile con Queso   40

Cilantro Dip   41

Colorful Cascarones   43

Creamy Chipotle Dip   44

Fiesta Dip   45

Flaming Cheese   46

Guacamole   47

Ham and Cheese Stacks   48

Jicama Ceviche   49

Mama's Queso   50

Nachos a la Butler   51

Seven-Layer Mexican Bean Dip   52

Sour Cream Nachos   53

Spicy Avocado Spread   54

Summer Chalupas   55

Texas Caviar   56

ACAPULCO-STYLE CEVICHE

When my brother and sister and I were younger, our family used to spend vacation time in Acapulco. If we were lying by the pool or on the beach, our lunch was always ceviche. With tons of fresh lime juice squeezed over it and as much hot sauce as we could stand, it was a staple of our diet.

Serves 8 to 10

Juice of 1 lime

3 pounds cod or other firm white fish fillets (such as orange
    roughy), rinsed, patted dry, and cut into 1-inch cubes

2 tomatoes, finely diced

2 tablespoons tomato sauce

1½ cups finely chopped onion

1 bunch cilantro, tough stems removed, finely chopped

One 14-ounce bottle pitted green olives, chopped

¼ cup liquid from canned jalapeño *chiles*

2 tablespoons olive oil

1 tablespoon dried oregano

Salt and pepper to taste

Tabasco sauce

1 Hass avocado, peeled, pitted, and thinly sliced

1 lime, cut into wedges

---

1. Combine 4 quarts salted water and the lime juice in a large pot and bring to a boil. Add the fish and cook for 1 minute. Drain well and set aside.

---

2. Combine the tomatoes, tomato sauce, onion, cilantro, olives, *chile* liquid, oil, and oregano

in a large bowl, mixing well. Gently stir the fish into the mixture, being careful not to break up the fish. Season with salt and pepper. Cover and marinate overnight in the refrigerator.

3. Transfer the ceviche to a serving bowl. Sprinkle with a few drops of Tabasco, and top with the avocado. Serve with the lime wedges on the side.

AVOCADO COCKTAIL

At Los Barrios, we call avocados "green gold," because they are so expensive. But when you taste them in our appetizers, you will think you've struck gold!

Serves 4 to 6

4 Hass avocados, peeled, pitted, and cut into 1-inch cubes

Juice of 2 lemons

2 tablespoons white vinegar

1½ cups ketchup

1 tablespoon Tabasco sauce

Salt and pepper to taste

1. Combine all the ingredients in a medium bowl, mixing well. Cover and refrigerate for 4 hours to blend the flavors.

2. Serve chilled, with crostini, crackers, or Tortilla Chips (see page 12).

AVOCADO MINI TAPAS

These little appetizers are simple and delicious, and very easy to prepare for last-minute guests. You can make them a bit fancier by using slices of crusty French bread instead of crackers. You could also serve the avocado mixture as a side salad. We learned to make these in my mother's hometown, Bustamante, in Nuevo León, Mexico. Avocado trees grew in my grandfather's backyard, and we would pick them and make all kinds of avocado "inventions." This is one of my favorites.

Makes 3 dozen

1 cup diced Hass avocado

1 tomato, chopped

¼ cup chopped onion

1 tablespoon lemon juice

½ teaspoon garlic powder

¼ cup salsa, homemade (see pages 7 and 10) or store-bought

36 crackers or tortilla chips, homemade (see page 12) or store-bought

4 slices bacon, cooked and crumbled (optional)

1. Combine the avocado, tomato, onion, lemon juice, garlic powder, and salsa in a small bowl, mixing well.

2. Spoon 1 rounded teaspoonful of the avocado mixture onto each cracker. Sprinkle with the bacon, if desired, and serve immediately.

BEACHFRONT VEGGIES

These fresh vegetables are great for munching on at the pool or beach. They make a healthy snack at any time.

Serves 4 to 6

1 jicama, peeled and cut into 2-inch-long sticks

6 carrots, peeled and cut into 2- to 3-inch-long sticks

2 cucumbers, peeled, halved, seeded, and cut into 2-inch-long sticks

2 limes, cut into quarters

Pure ground *chile* powder to taste (see Note)

1. Arrange the vegetables on a platter. Squeeze the juice of the limes over the top and sprinkle with *chile* powder.

2. Cover and refrigerate. Serve chilled.

NOTE: Pure ground *chile* powder can be found at Latin markets and some larger supermarkets.

These are great with ranch dressing or a creamy vinaigrette. Another alternative is 1 cup sour cream blended with ½ cup Los Barrios Salsa (see page 7).

BEEF OR CHICKEN EMPANADAS

Makes 10 empanadas

> 3 cups all-purpose flour
>
> 1½ teaspoons baking powder
>
> Pinch of salt
>
> ½ cup vegetable shortening
>
> ¾ cup warm water
>
> 1½ cups shredded cooked chicken or Picadillo (see page 129)
>
> 10 to 12 green olives, pitted and finely chopped

1. Combine the flour, baking powder, and salt in a large bowl. Add the shortening and mix together until a course meal forms. Add the water and mix until well blended. Divide the dough into 10 pieces and shape into balls about the size of a golf ball.

2. Preheat the oven to 325°F.

3. On a floured surface, using a floured rolling pin, roll out each ball of dough into a 4-inch round. Put about 2 tablespoons of the chicken on one side of each round. Sprinkle about 1 teaspoon of the olives over the chicken, and fold the dough over to make a half-moon-shaped turnover. Pinch the edges of the dough together to seal.

4. Arrange the empanadas on a greased baking sheet and bake for 12 to 15 minutes, or until golden brown. Serve warm.

NOTE: You can deep-fry the empanadas rather than bake them. Fry in hot oil, in batches, until golden brown, about 1½ minutes on each side.

The empanadas can be assembled ahead of time and frozen for up to 1 month. To reheat, bake at 325°F for 15 minutes, or until golden brown. Serve with Guacamole (see page 47) and Los Barrios Salsa (see page 7).

CEVICHE COCKTAIL

Serves 6 to 8

2 pounds cod, red snapper, or orange roughy fillets, rinsed,
   patted dry, and cut into 1-inch cubes

1½ cups lime juice

1 onion, finely diced

12 green olives, pitted and diced

2 to 3 serrano *chiles* (to taste), finely chopped (optional)

½ cup finely chopped cilantro

1 teaspoon dried oregano, or to taste

½ cup mineral water

2 tablespoons olive oil

Juice of 1 orange

One 14-ounce bottle ketchup

Salt and pepper to taste

---

1. Put the fish in a glass baking dish or shallow bowl and add the lime juice, making sure all the pieces of fish are covered. Cover and marinate overnight in the refrigerator.

---

2. Combine the onion, olives, *chiles,* if using, cilantro, oregano, mineral water, olive oil, orange juice, and ketchup in a large bowl, stirring to blend well. Season with salt and pepper. Add the fish and stir gently to coat. Refrigerate for at least 2 hours.

---

3. Serve in individual bowls or glasses, with crackers or Tortilla Chips (see page 12).

VARIATION: Instead of marinating the fish, you can cook it in a large pot of boiling salted water, with the juice of 1 lime, for 1 minute; drain well and proceed as directed.

CHICHARRÓN DE QUESO

Serves 4

2 cups shredded Manchego cheese

4 flour tortillas, homemade (see page 6) or store-bought,
   warmed

½ cup Green Tomatillo Sauce (see page 119)

1. Heat a stovetop grill or large skillet until very hot. Place the cheese on the grill in 4 rounds and heat until melted. When the cheese has melted, blot with paper towels to absorb the excess fat. Fold each round over to form a half-moon shape.

2. Place the cheese in the tortillas, top with the sauce, and fold the tortillas over.

Makes 3 cups

2½ pounds Velveeta or smooth-melt cheese, cut into small cubes

8 to 10 canned jalapeño *chiles* (to taste), sliced

¼ cup water

---

1. Put the cheese in a large heavy skillet and heat over low to medium-low heat, stirring constantly, until it begins to melt. Stir in the *chiles*. Reduce the heat to very low and gradually add the water, stirring constantly until the cheese is melted and smooth; be careful not to scorch the cheese.

---

2. Transfer to a slow-cooker, a chafing dish over a flame, or a warm serving bowl. Serve immediately, with Tortilla Chips (see page 12), crackers, or cut-up raw vegetables.

CILANTRO DIP

Makes 2½ cups

1 cup sour cream

One 8-ounce package cream cheese, at room temperature

½ cup mayonnaise

1 bunch cilantro, tough stems removed, finely chopped

3 serrano *chiles,* finely chopped

3 scallions, chopped

Dash of soy sauce

1. Combine all the ingredients in a blender and blend until thoroughly mixed. Transfer to a serving bowl, or shape into a ball and place on a plate. Cover and refrigerate for 2 hours.

2. Serve with Tortilla Chips (see page 12), crackers, or cut-up raw vegetables.

VARIATION: To make Cilantro Mousse, add one 7-gram package unflavored gelatin, dissolved in ½ cup water, to the mixture. Put it into a 1-quart mold, cover, and refrigerate overnight.

In our family, we love to celebrate any occasion, whether it is a birthday, a promotion, or a fiesta. You can be sure that our events are full of fun, laughter, *great food,* and plenty of *cascarones.* What is a *cascarón,* you ask? It's a great big party favor! *Cascarones,* confetti-filled eggs, have been around for years. They are a gesture of friendship, and they are very much a part of any event in San Antonio. How do you handle them? Very gently! Tradition has it that you walk up to a friend, and without letting that person know what you are about to do, you gently crack the egg open on his or her head, letting the confetti fly freely. A "nice" way of breaking a *cascarón* is to crack it in your hand and then pour the contents over the head of the intended. *Cascarones* are a lot of fun. Some of my cousins always have at least a hundred dozen eggs at their celebrations. Everyone joins in the fun, young and old—no one escapes.

When I did a cooking segment with Emeril Lagasse for *Good Morning America,* I introduced him to *cascarones.* He commented, "I've seen a lot of things done with eggs, but never have I had this much fun enjoying them!" When Bobby Flay came to town for his *Food Nation* show, he asked, "What's with the purple eggs?" He was immediately introduced to *cascarones* by my children. He never asked that question again. Start saving those eggshells.

COLORFUL CASCARONES

3 cups water

4 teaspoons vinegar

4 different colors liquid food color

3 dozen eggshells (see Note), thoroughly rinsed
    and dried

2½ cups confetti

Thirty-six 2-inch squares tissue paper (you can
    also use old comic strips or wrapping paper)

Glue

1. Bring the water to a boil. Divide the boiling water among 4 disposable cups. Add
   1 teaspoon vinegar and 20 drops of a different food color to each cup, stirring
   to blend. One at a time, place the eggshells in the cups and turn them constantly
   until evenly colored, 3 to 4 minutes (color 9 eggshells in each color). Transfer to a
   newspaper-lined counter to dry.

2. Fill each eggshell with 1 tablespoon of the confetti. Spread some glue around the
   opening of the shell, and cover with a tissue-paper square to seal, pressing down the
   edges.

VARIATION: Instead of dying the eggs, you can just decorate them using colored
markers. For a more special effect, spread some glue on the tissue-paper tops and sprinkle more confetti over them.

NOTE: To collect eggshells, instead of cracking them open when you are cooking
with eggs, use a sharp paring knife to cut off the top of each egg, making a quarter-sized
hole. Discard the top piece of shell. Thoroughly rinse and dry the eggshells and reserve
them for your cascarones.

CREAMY CHIPOTLE DIP

Serves 6 to 8

1 pound Velveeta cheese, cut into 1-inch cubes

¼ cup chopped canned chipotle *chiles*

2 cups sour cream

1. Melt the cheese in a large heavy saucepan over medium-low heat, stirring until smooth. Gradually stir in the *chiles*.

2. Remove from the heat and stir in the sour cream until well blended. Serve immediately.

Enjoy this dip with Tortilla Chips (see page 12) or cut-up raw vegetables.

FIESTA DIP

In San Antonio, we celebrate Fiesta every April. It is ten days of fun, frolic, and family. This dip reminds us that Fiesta is not just one week out of the year, but anytime and anywhere you want it to be. As we say in San Antonio, *"¡Viva Fiesta!"*

Makes 6 cups

1 pound ground beef

½ onion, finely chopped

One 10¾-ounce can cream of mushroom soup

One 10¾-ounce can cream of chicken soup

2¼ cups enchilada sauce, homemade (see page 3) or store-bought

1 pound Velveeta cheese, cut into 1-inch cubes

6 to 7 canned jalapeño *chiles* (to taste), finely chopped

Salt and pepper to taste

1. Sauté the beef in a large heavy skillet over medium heat until browned and cooked through, 7 to 8 minutes. Drain the fat from the pan.

2. Add the onion, both soups, and the sauce to the pan and cook, stirring often, until well blended and hot. Gradually add the cheese, allowing the cubes to melt before you add the next batch. Add the *chiles* and season with salt and pepper. Reduce the heat to low and cook for 4 to 5 minutes longer.

3. Transfer to a slow-cooker or a chafing dish set over a flame, and serve.

This dip can be enjoyed with chips or spooned over tamales, baked potatoes, or even scrambled eggs. Want a fun way to serve the dip? Cut an individual bag of Fritos open down one side. Spoon some dip into the bag and enjoy, à la Frito pie.

FLAMING CHEESE

Queso Flameado

This is one of the favorite appetizers at the restaurant. We serve it in a miniature cast-iron skillet. We heat the skillet, add the cheese and chorizo mixture, and pour a splash of 151-proof liquor over the cheese. Then we ignite it—although the flames die down after a couple of seconds, the dish creates a lot of excitement as it is carried to the table. But the best part is the taste. Please be very careful when you prepare this at home.

Serves 2 to 4

¼ pound chorizo (Mexican sausage), casings removed

½ onion, thinly sliced

1 small tomato, diced

¼ cup sliced mushrooms (optional)

1 serrano *chile,* minced (optional)

2 cups shredded *queso Chihuahua* or Monterey Jack cheese

2 tablespoons 151-proof liquor, such as Everclear

1. Preheat the oven to 350°F.

2. Brown the sausage in a large skillet over medium heat, 5 to 6 minutes. Pour off the fat. Add the onion, tomato, and mushrooms and/or *chile,* if using, and sauté until softened, 3 to 4 minutes. Remove from the heat.

3. Meanwhile, spread the cheese in a small baking dish and bake for 5 to 10 minutes, until completely melted. Remove from the oven.

4. Pour the chorizo mixture over the cheese. Pour the liquor over the top, and using a long match, carefully ignite the liquor—the flames will die down in 30 to 45 seconds. Serve with tortillas made from corn or flour tortillas (see page 4 or 6) by placing the cheese inside each tortilla and folding them over to form a taco.

GUACAMOLE ✴

Mmm! Guacamole! You can dip into it, spread it, scoop it up, or dollop it on top of just about anything. You can do so many things with guacamole—and it's always a favorite.

Makes 2 to 3 cups

4 Hass avocados
1 teaspoon garlic powder
Salt and pepper to taste

1. Slice the avocados lengthwise in half and remove the pits. Using a spoon, scoop the avocado flesh into a bowl. Using a potato masher or a fork, mash the avocado, making it as chunky or as smooth as you like.

2. Season with the garlic powder and salt and pepper. Serve chilled or at room temperature.

VARIATIONS: You can add chopped onion, chopped serrano or roasted poblano *chiles* (see page 79), chopped cilantro, and/or diced tomatoes for different flavors.

HAM AND CHEESE STACKS

Sincronizadas de Jamón

*C*hildren love these little stacks (made without the *chile* pepper, of course). Adults, too, will enjoy them, as an appetizer or a snack.

Makes 16 wedges

4 slices ham

12 corn tortillas, homemade (see page 4) or store-bought

4 slices *queso Chihuahua* or Monterey Jack cheese

3 tomatoes

¼ onion, coarsely chopped

1 serrano *chile,* coarsely chopped

1½ tablespoons vegetable oil

1 cup water

1. Place a slice of ham on a tortilla, cover with a second tortilla, and top with a slice of cheese. Cover with a third tortilla, and secure the edges with toothpicks. Repeat with the remaining ham, tortillas, and cheese.

2. Preheat a grill, or heat a heavy medium skillet over medium-high heat. Grill the tomatoes, or heat in the skillet, for 12 to 15 minutes, turning occasionally, until they are blackened. Transfer to a blender, add the onion and *chile,* and blend for 1 to 2 minutes.

3. Heat the oil in a large saucepan over medium heat. Add the tomato mixture and the water, bring to a simmer, and simmer for 3 to 4 minutes. Reduce the heat and carefully place one stack of layered tortillas in the sauce, making sure it is submerged. Heat until the cheese is melted, about 2 minutes. Remove from the sauce, remove the toothpicks, and cut into quarters. Repeat with remaining stacks. Serve hot.

JICAMA CEVICHE

Serves 8

4 jicamas, peeled and cut into small dice

1 cup lime juice

1 onion, finely diced

12 green olives, pitted and diced

2 to 3 serrano *chiles* (to taste), finely chopped (optional)

¼ cup finely chopped cilantro

1 tablespoon dried oregano

2 tablespoons olive oil

Juice of 1 orange

½ cup mineral water

1¼ cups ketchup

Salt and pepper to taste

1. Place the jicama in a glass baking dish or shallow bowl and add the lime juice. Cover and marinate overnight in the refrigerator.

2. Combine the onion, olives, *chiles*, if using, cilantro, oregano, oil, orange juice, mineral water, and ketchup in a medium bowl, stirring to blend. Season with salt and pepper. Stir in the jicama. Cover and refrigerate for 3 to 4 hours.

3. Serve chilled, with crackers or Tortilla Chips (see page 12).

MAMA'S QUESO

This is one of my mom's favorite dishes, and when she prepares it, we all come running. It brings back many memories of visits to her hometown in Mexico. Every once in a while, someone from Bustamante will come into the restaurant and bring her some fresh Mexican cheese. You can be certain that the first dish she prepares will be this one.

Makes 2 cups

2 tablespoons vegetable oil

¼ onion, thinly sliced

2 to 3 serrano *chiles* (to taste), chopped

4 tomatoes, halved and grated on the large holes of a
    box grater

¼ cup water

8 ounces *queso Chihuahua,* asadero, or Monterey Jack cheese,
    cut into small chunks

Salt to taste

1. Heat the oil in a large skillet over medium-high heat. Add the onion and *chiles* and cook until softened, 2 to 3 minutes. Add the tomatoes and water and bring to a boil. Reduce the heat and simmer for about 8 minutes.

2. Gradually add the cheese to the skillet, allowing each batch to melt before you add the next. Stir to blend well and remove from the heat. Season with salt, and serve hot.

NACHOS A LA BUTLER ✴

As I mentioned earlier, these nachos were named for the man who invented the combination. He no longer lives in the United States, but he always shares a meal or two with us when he comes back to San Antonio to visit. Make these in batches, and have a batch ready to pop in the oven when the first one comes out—once you try them, you'll want more.

Serves 6 to 8

> 36 tortilla chips, homemade (see page 12) or store-bought
>
> 2½ cups refried beans, homemade (see page 163)
>   or store-bought
>
> 1 pound ground beef, cooked
>
> 4 cups shredded American or Cheddar cheese
>
> 1 cup Guacamole (see page 47)
>
> 1 onion, finely chopped
>
> 2 tomatoes, diced
>
> 1 jalapeño *chile,* sliced

1. If using a conventional oven rather than a microwave, preheat it to 350°F.

2. Spread the tortilla chips on 2 microwavable or ovenproof platters or large plates. Spread the beans on top of the chips and top with the ground beef. Sprinkle with the cheese.

3. Place 1 plate in the microwave and heat for 30 seconds, or until the cheese has melted. Or place the plate in the preheated oven and heat for 3 to 5 minutes. Place dollops of half of the guacamole over the nachos and top with half of the onion, tomatoes, and *chile.* Serve immediately, and repeat with the second plate of nachos.

SEVEN-LAYER MEXICAN BEAN DIP

This dip has become so popular, you can even find it in the deli section of grocery stores in San Antonio. What makes our version stand out are the homemade refried beans and guacamole. Feel free to add other ingredients, such as 2 cups cooked ground beef or shredded cooked chicken.

Serves 12 to 15

2 cups refried beans, homemade (see page 163) or store-bought

2 cups Guacamole (see page 47)

2 cups sour cream

3 tomatoes, diced

2 onions, diced

1½ cups shredded *queso Chihuahua* or Monterey Jack cheese

1½ cups shredded American cheese

1 cup chopped black olives (optional)

1. Spread the beans evenly over the bottom of a 9 by 13-inch baking dish. Cover and refrigerate for 10 to 15 minutes, until slightly chilled.

2. Using a rubber spatula, spread the guacamole evenly over the beans. Spread the sour cream evenly over the guacamole. Scatter the tomatoes evenly over the guacamole, then scatter the onions over the tomatoes. Combine the cheeses in a medium bowl, tossing to mix, and sprinkle over the top of the tomatoes. Add olives on top, if desired. Refrigerate for at least an hour.

3. Serve with Tortilla Chips (see page 12).

This dip also goes great with flautas, or serve it as a side dish with Steak Fajitas with Citrus Marinade (see page 139).

SOUR CREAM NACHOS

Nachos Agrios

If you are addicted to sour cream, then make these as often as necessary to satisfy your indulgence.

Serves 6 to 8

36 tortilla chips, homemade (see page 12) or store-bought

2½ cups refried beans, homemade (see page 163)
    or store-bought

1 cup grated Swiss cheese

1 cup grated provolone cheese

¾ cup finely chopped jalapeño *chiles*

1½ cups sour cream

¾ cup finely chopped pimientos

---

1. Preheat the oven to 300°F.

---

2. Arrange the tortilla chips on an ovenproof platter. Spread a layer of the beans on each chip. Combine the cheeses and scatter generously over the beans. Sprinkle the *chiles* over the cheese. Bake for about 2 minutes, or until the cheese is melted.

---

3. Top each nacho with a dollop of sour cream. Garnish with the pimientos, and serve immediately.

SPICY AVOCADO SPREAD

Makes 4 cups

One 8-ounce package cream cheese, at room temperature

1 cup sour cream

1 Hass avocado, peeled, pitted, and sliced

One 4-ounce can sliced jalapeño *chiles,* with their liquid,
     plus extra for garnish

10 green olives, pitted and chopped

1. Combine the cream cheese, sour cream, avocado, and *chiles,* with their liquid, in a blender and blend until smooth. If the mixture seems too thick, add a little more jalapeño liquid.

2. Transfer to a serving bowl and cover the top with the olives and additional sliced *chiles.* Serve immediately.

Serve this with Tortilla Chips (see page 12), crackers, or raw vegetables.

SUMMER CHALUPAS

I first had these chalupas at a birthday party and immediately fell in love. I promptly went home and served them to my family. They loved them too. We call them "summer chalupas" because they are perfect to serve when it's hot. They're easy to make, light, and a great appetizer.

Makes 8 mini chalupas

2 cups refried beans, homemade (see page 163)
   or store-bought
8 mini chalupa shells (see Note)
2 cups shredded cooked chicken
4 cups shredded cabbage
1½ cups crumbled *queso añejo* (crumbly white
   Mexican cheese) or feta cheese
¾ cup sour cream
1 tomato, diced

1. Spread the beans in the chalupa shells. Top with the chicken, cabbage, and cheese.

2. Top each chalupa with a dollop of sour cream, and garnish with the tomato. Easy as that!

NOTE: Mini chalupa shells (approximately 3 inches in diameter) can be found at Latin markets.

TEXAS CAVIAR

Everything about Texas is special, so why not our own style of "caviar"? It isn't as expensive as other caviars, but it tastes great. And, in true Texas fashion, the recipe makes enough to serve a small army. We love making this for Super Bowl Sunday.

Makes 3½ quarts

Two 16-ounce cans black beans, drained

One 16-ounce can garbanzo beans (chickpeas), drained

One 16-ounce can corn kernels, drained

Two 4-ounce cans diced green *chiles*

One 32-ounce jar prepared salsa (see Note)

10 tomatoes, diced

1 green bell pepper, diced

1 red onion, diced

1 jicama, peeled and diced

2 to 3 garlic cloves, finely chopped

1 bunch cilantro, tough stems removed, finely chopped

Juice of 4 to 5 limes (to taste)

3 Hass avocados, peeled, pitted, and cut into ½-inch dice

1. Combine all the ingredients in a large bowl.

2. Cover and refrigerate for several hours to blend the flavors. Bring to room temperature before serving with tortilla chips.

NOTE: We like to make this spicy, so we use our own homemade Los Barrios Salsa (see page 7). Using store-bought ingredients makes the recipe easier, but you can always go for fresh, homemade ingredients instead.

SOUPS

Butternut Squash Soup   59

Creamy Bean Soup   61

Hearty Beef and Vegetable Soup   62

Hot and Spicy Tlalpeño-Style Soup   64

Mama Viola's Chicken Rice Soup   66

Menudo   67

Spicy Tomato Soup with

Meatballs and Cilantro   69

Tortilla Soup   71

Vermicelli Tomato Soup   73

BUTTERNUT SQUASH SOUP

This is a delicious soup for fall. I first tried it at my friend Becky's house and loved it on the spot. I asked her to share the recipe with me, and now I will share it with you.

Serves 6 to 8

2 tablespoons butter

1 onion, chopped

2 cups chicken broth

1 pound butternut squash, peeled, seeded, and cut into 1-inch cubes

2 pears, peeled, cored, and sliced

1 teaspoon chopped fresh thyme

¼ teaspoon salt

¼ teaspoon white pepper

¼ teaspoon ground coriander

1 cup heavy cream

½ cup chopped toasted pecans (see box on page 60)

1. Melt the butter in a 4-quart Dutch oven or other heavy pot over medium heat. Add the onion and sauté until softened, 4 to 5 minutes. Stir in the broth, squash, two thirds of the pears (toss remaining pears with lemon juice so they don't discolor), the thyme, salt, white pepper, and coriander. Bring to a boil, then reduce the heat to medium, cover, and simmer until the squash is tender, 10 to 15 minutes.

2. Transfer half of the soup to a blender and blend until smooth. Pour into a bowl and repeat with the remaining soup. Return the soup to the pot and heat over low heat until hot. Stir in the cream and heat through, stirring frequently. Ladle into bowls and garnish with the reserved pears and the pecans.

To toast nuts, spread them in a single layer on a baking sheet and toast in a preheated 350°F oven, stirring occasionally, until lightly browned, 8 to 10 minutes.

CREAMY BEAN SOUP

Sopa de Frijol

Need a great soup to warm up a cold day? Sopa de Frijol is your answer. **Traditionally prepared in Monterrey, the recipe comes from my aunt. We tweaked it a bit, and voilà! I like mine served with a little lime juice squeezed into it.**

Serves 12

4 cups Traditional Pot of Beans (see page 168)

6 cups chicken broth

6 tablespoons (¾ stick) butter

3 cups half-and-half

1 cup heavy cream

¾ teaspoon salt

2 onions, chopped

1 cup croutons

1 cup grated mozzarella cheese

1 bunch cilantro, tough stems removed, finely chopped

1. In batches, combine the beans and broth in a blender and blend to a puree.

2. Melt the butter in a large soup pot over medium heat. Add the pureed beans, half-and-half, cream, and salt and bring to a boil.

3. Ladle into bowls, and garnish with the onions, croutons, cheese, and cilantro.

HEARTY BEEF AND VEGETABLE SOUP

Caldo de Res

Every morning, when the kitchen staff arrives, they follow the same routine. Part of that routine involves putting the *caldo* (soup) on. We make this *caldo* fresh every morning, and by one o'clock in the afternoon, it is always gone. We have plenty of *caldo* fans who arrive early for lunch to make sure they get some of the soup.

Serves 6

5 pounds stew bones

¼ cup plus 2 tablespoons salt

¼ cup garlic powder

4 ears corn, husked and cut in half

6 celery stalks, cut into ½-inch slices

3 carrots, peeled and cut into 1-inch chunks

4 potatoes, peeled and cut into 2-inch chunks

3 tomatoes, cut into wedges

3 zucchini, cut into 2-inch chunks

2 onions, each cut into 6 wedges

½ head cabbage, cut into quarters

1 green bell pepper, sliced

6 cups hot Spanish Rice (see page 165)

1 lemon, cut into 6 wedges

----

1. Put the bones in a large stockpot, add water to cover by 6 inches, and bring to a boil. Boil gently for 45 minutes.

----

2. Stir in the salt and garlic powder, then add the corn, celery, and carrots. Boil for another 15

minutes, then add the potatoes, tomatoes, zucchini, onion, cabbage, and bell pepper. Boil for 15 minutes longer.

---

3. Ladle the soup into 6 large bowls. Add 1 cup of the rice to each bowl, and squeeze the juice from a lemon wedge over each. Serve immediately.

HOT AND SPICY TLALPEÑO-STYLE SOUP

Caldo Tlalpeño

Serves 4 to 6

SOUP

One whole 2½- to 3-pound fryer chicken, cut into 8 to 10 pieces

½ onion

1 head garlic

6 quarts water

1 cup cooked or canned garbanzo beans (chickpeas)

2 carrots, peeled and diced

GARNISH

1 Hass avocado, peeled, pitted, and diced

¾ cup shredded *queso Chihuahua* or Monterey Jack cheese

2 canned chipotle *chiles,* diced (see Note)

½ cup chopped onion

½ cup chopped cilantro

---

1. Put the chicken, onion, and garlic in a large pot and add the water. Bring to a boil, reduce the heat, and simmer until the chicken is cooked through, skimming off any scum that forms on top, about 30 minutes.

---

2. Remove the chicken from the pot and let cool slightly. Remove the meat from the bones, discarding the skin and bones, and shred into bite-sized pieces. Strain the broth and return it to the pot. Add the chicken, beans, and carrots to the broth and bring to a boil. Boil gently for 15 minutes (prepare the garnish while the vegetables cook).

---

3. Arrange the avocado, cheese, *chiles,* chopped onion, and cilantro in separate mounds on a serving plate. Ladle the soup into bowls, and pass the plate of garnishes so everyone can garnish his or her own bowl as desired.

N O T E : Traditionally, the chipotles are added to the broth to make it spicy, but since the *chiles* can be quite hot, we like to allow our guests to add them individually, at their discretion.

MAMA VIOLA'S CHICKEN RICE SOUP

Caldo de Pollo

Serves 4

One 2½- to 3-pound fryer chicken, cut into 8 to 10 pieces

1 tablespoon salt

8 cloves garlic

1 cup white rice

2 carrots, peeled and cut into ¼- to ½-inch slices

3 celery stalks, cut into ¼-inch slices

2 potatoes, peeled and cut into 2-inch cubes

1 onion, sliced

2 tomatoes, sliced

One 14-ounce can garbanzo beans (chickpeas), peeled

½ bunch cilantro, tough stems removed, finely chopped

Lemon wedges for garnish

1. Put the chicken in a large pot and add water to cover by 3 inches. Add the salt, garlic, and rice and bring to a boil. Boil for 30 minutes, skimming off any scum that forms on top.

2. Add the carrots, celery, and potatoes and cook for another 20 minutes, or until the chicken is cooked. Stir in the onion, tomatoes, beans, and cilantro.

3. Ladle into bowls and garnish with the lemon wedges. Serve with warm corn tortillas (see page 4).

MENUDO (TRIPE SOUP)

JM*enudo* **(from the Spanish word for tripe) is known as** *the* **cure for hang-overs! It is always served at midnight at** *tornabodas,* **the late-night party that follows a wedding. They usually last for two to three hours, but in some cases can go on all night. They are the time when the two families of the new couple finally get a chance to relax and get a bite to eat.**

Makes 10 to 12 servings

SOUP

5 pounds beef tripe, cut into 1- to 2-inch squares

2 pounds pig's feet (optional)

¼ onion, diced

3 garlic cloves

1½ tablespoons salt

3 quarts water

3 ancho *chiles* or ¼ cup pure ground *chile* powder
    (available at Latin markets and some larger
    supermarkets)

2 cups hominy

1½ tablespoons dried oregano

GARNISH

1 cup diced onion

2 lemons, cut into 8 wedges each

1. Put the tripe, pig's feet, if using, onion, garlic, and salt in a large stockpot and add the water. Bring to a simmer over medium heat and cook until the tripe is tender, about 3 hours.

2. Meanwhile, if using ancho *chiles,* put them in a small saucepan, add water to cover, and bring to a boil. Boil until softened, about 10 minutes. Drain and let cool slightly, then peel off the skin. Put the *chiles* in a blender and puree.

3. Add the pureed *chiles* (or the *chile* powder), hominy, and oregano to the soup. Reduce the heat to low, and cook for another 30 minutes

4. Ladle the soup into bowls, and serve with the onion and lemon on the side, along with tortillas (see box). One tablespoon of diced onion should be stirred into each bowl of soup, and the juice of the lemons added to taste.

Some of our diners also request finely chopped serrano chiles *to garnish their* menudo. *Warm corn or flour tortillas (see page 4 or 6) are a must with* menudo.

SPICY TOMATO SOUP WITH MEATBALLS AND CILANTRO

Sopa de Albóndigas con Cilantro

This recipe came to our family from a cousin in my mother's hometown of Bustamante, in Nuevo León, Mexico. She had a big pot of the soup waiting for us when we arrived for a visit. It has since become the standard welcome for us anytime we have the chance to get away and visit that charming *pueblo*.

Serves 6

MEATBALLS

2½ pounds ground beef

2 eggs

½ cup white rice

1 tablespoon all-purpose flour

½ teaspoon salt

¼ teaspoon pepper

¼ teaspoon garlic powder

¼ teaspoon ground cumin

SOUP

2½ quarts water

2 tablespoons vegetable oil

2 onions, sliced

2 tomatoes, sliced

6 serrano *chiles,* finely chopped

1 bunch cilantro, tough stems removed, finely chopped

---

1. To make the meatballs, combine the ground beef, eggs, ¼ cup of the rice, the flour, salt, pepper, garlic powder, and cumin in a large bowl, mixing well. Shape the mixture into meatballs about 1½ inches in diameter.

---

2. Bring the water to a boil in a large stockpot over high heat. Add the meatballs and the remaining ¼ cup rice and boil for 30 minutes, skimming off any scum that forms on top.

3. Meanwhile, heat the oil in a medium skillet over medium heat. Add the onions, tomatoes, and about one sixth of the *chiles* and sauté until the onion is softened, about 5 minutes.

4. Add the onion mixture to the meatballs and broth, along with the remaining *chiles,* reduce the heat to low, and simmer for 10 minutes. Just before serving, stir in the cilantro.

Serve the soup with Refried Beans (see page 163) and warm corn tortillas (see page 4).

TORTILLA SOUP

There are many versions of tortilla soup. Ours starts with a tomato base, then adds chicken, cheese, avocado, tortilla strips, and cilantro. It is a meal in itself, and just writing the recipe makes me hungry for it!

Serves 10 to 12

SOUP

2 tablespoons vegetable oil

1 large onion, sliced

2 bay leaves

10 peppercorns

9 tomatoes, cut in half

2 heads garlic

4 quarts water

1 chicken bouillon cube

3 drops Tabasco sauce, or to taste

1 teaspoon Worcestershire sauce, or to taste

Salt to taste

GARNISH

3 cups diced cooked chicken

2 Hass avocados, peeled, pitted, and sliced

2 cups crumbled *queso añejo* (crumbly white
    Mexican cheese) or feta cheese

Fried tortilla strips

3 tablespoons chopped cilantro

1. Heat the vegetable oil in a large stockpot over medium-high heat. Add the onion, bay leaves, and peppercorns and sauté until the onion is softened, 3 to 4 minutes. Add the tomatoes, garlic, and water and bring to a boil. Boil until the tomatoes are starting to fall apart, about 30 minutes.

2. Add the bouillon cube and cook for 20 minutes. Strain the soup into a large pot, pushing down on the solids with a potato masher or wooden spoon to force out all the juices. Discard the solids.

3. Bring the broth to a simmer over medium heat. Add the Tabasco sauce and Worcestershire, and season with salt. Ladle into bowls, and garnish with the chicken, avocados, cheese, fried tortilla strips, and cilantro.

VERMICELLI TOMATO SOUP

Fideo

Fideo is a dish that everyone's mother or grandmother prepared when they were growing up in Mexico and in San Antonio. I'm glad to say that I keep the tradition going in my family, and hope it brings back memories of Sunday dinner at *Abuelita*'s.

Serves 4

2 tablespoons vegetable oil

One 5-ounce box vermicelli

½ onion, thinly sliced

2 garlic cloves, finely chopped

1 green bell pepper, thinly sliced

2 to 3 tomatoes, cut in half

One 15-ounce can chicken broth

1 cup water

Salt to taste

1. Heat the oil in a large deep saucepan over low heat. Add the vermicelli and toss back and forth with 2 spoons until golden brown, 5 to 6 minutes; do not allow the noodles to burn. Add the onion, garlic, and bell pepper and cook until tender, about 5 minutes. Drain off the oil from the pan.

2. Meanwhile, put the tomatoes in a blender and blend to a puree.

3. Add the tomatoes to the vermicelli along with the broth and water, and bring to a simmer. Simmer gently for 10 to 15 minutes. Season with salt, and serve hot.

VARIATION: Add 1 cup peeled, diced potatoes to the soup along with the broth and water.

SALADS

Corn and Avocado Salad with
Green-Gold Dressing   77
Cuernavaca Salad with
Honey-Mustard Vinaigrette   78
Fresh Tomato Salad   80
Los Valles Fruit Cup   81
Louie's Salad   82
Mango Salad   83
Red, Green, and Yellow Pepper Salad   84
San Antonio Chicken Salad   85
Spicy Jell-O Vegetable Salad   86

CORN AND AVOCADO SALAD WITH GREEN-GOLD DRESSING

Serves 6

DRESSING

2 Hass avocados, peeled, pitted, and cut into chunks

1 tablespoon chopped onion

2 tablespoons olive oil

2 tablespoons white vinegar

2 tablespoons water

1½ teaspoons lemon juice

1½ teaspoons Worcestershire sauce

3 drops Tabasco sauce, or to taste

2 teaspoons salt

½ teaspoon sugar

⅛ teaspoon chili powder

SALAD

4 Hass avocados, peeled, pitted, and cut into 1-inch cubes

1½ cups canned corn kernels, drained

2 tablespoons finely chopped parsley

6 cups torn romaine lettuce leaves or bibb lettuce

1. To make the dressing, combine all the ingredients in a blender and blend until creamy.

2. Combine the avocados, corn, and parsley in a medium bowl. Add the dressing and toss to mix thoroughly. Cover and refrigerate for 4 hours.

3. To serve, line a large platter with the lettuce, and mound the salad in the center.

CUERNAVACA SALAD WITH HONEY-MUSTARD VINAIGRETTE

Serves 4 to 6

SALAD

12 romaine lettuce leaves

2 tomatoes, sliced, then each slice cut in half

1 Hass avocado, peeled, pitted, and cut into ¾-inch-thick slices

1 poblano *chile,* roasted (see box), peeled, seeded, and sliced

2 cups grated *queso Chihuahua* or Monterey Jack cheese

VINAIGRETTE

1 cup olive oil

3 to 4 tablespoons lime juice

2 teaspoons mustard

2 teaspoons honey

Salt and pepper to taste

1. Line a platter with the lettuce leaves. Arrange the tomatoes on the lettuce, followed by the avocado and *chile,* and scatter the cheese over the top. Cover and refrigerate for 1 to 2 hours, until chilled.

2. Meanwhile, make the vinaigrette: Combine all the ingredients in a jar, close tightly, and shake until well blended.

3. Serve the salad chilled, with the dressing on the side.

To roast poblano *chiles:* Preheat the oven to 350°F. Lightly brush the *chiles* with vegetable oil and place on a cookie sheet. Roast for about 30 minutes, turning the *chiles* every 10 minutes, until the skin begins to split and peel. Place the *chiles* in a plastic bag, seal, and let cool and steam until thoroughly cooled. When the peppers are cool, peel off the thin skin. Cut them lengthwise in half, and remove the seeds and membranes.

You can also do this on the stovetop instead of in the oven. Place the peppers in a large skillet over medium to high heat and cook, turning them every 10 minutes, until the skin begins to split and peel, about 30 minutes; the peppers will darken in color. Peel and clean the peppers as directed above.

To roast bell peppers: Slice bell peppers in half. Place skin side up in a preheated broiler. Broil for 6 to 8 minutes, until skin is charred. Remove from broiler, place peppers in a bowl, cover with plastic wrap, and let cool. Carefully peel off skins and slice as desired.

FRESH TOMATO SALAD

These tomatoes make a great side dish for any summer party. Served chilled, they complement many dishes. And the salad is versatile; you can top it with fresh lime juice, or use your favorite vinaigrette or Italian dressing made with balsamic vinegar. My sister-in-law, Traci, prepares this salad for all our family events.

Serves 6 to 8

4 beefsteak tomatoes, cut into ¼-inch-thick slices

2 cups crumbled *queso fresco* (crumbly white
      Mexican cheese) or feta cheese

½ cup chopped scallions

2 limes, halved

½ cup finely chopped cilantro

Salt and pepper to taste

1. Arrange the tomatoes on a large serving platter. Scatter the cheese and scallions over them.

2. Squeeze the juice from the limes over the salad. Sprinkle with the cilantro, and season with salt and pepper.

3. Cover and refrigerate for 1 hour before serving.

LOS VALLES FRUIT CUP

If you've ever been to Mexico, you know that on just about every street corner, there is a vendor of some sort. Some sell souvenirs; others cook some of the best hot dogs I've ever had. The variety of food they sell is endless. One of my favorites is the fresh fruit stand. Fortunately for the people of San Antonio, fresh fruit stands have arrived here. I particularly like the Frutería Los Valles on West Avenue, run by a wonderful family. Here I share a little of what they are about.

Serves 4 to 6

1 pineapple, peeled, cored, and cut into 1-inch cubes

5 mangoes, peeled, pitted, and cut into 1-inch cubes

½ small watermelon, seeded and flesh cut into 1-inch cubes

1 cantaloupe, halved, seeded, and flesh cut into 1-inch cubes

1 pint strawberries, washed, hulled, and quartered

Juice of 2 limes, or to taste

Pure ground *chile* powder for fruits and vegetables

(see Note) to taste

1. Combine the fruit in a large bowl. Drizzle the lime juice over the top, then sprinkle with *chile* powder.

2. Cover and refrigerate. Serve chilled.

N O T E : Some specialty markets and most Latin groceries sell a *chile* powder that is specifically for fruits and vegetables. It adds a sweet but spicy flavor; you may want to use it sparingly at first, but you will soon find it addictive.

LOUIE'S SALAD ✺

Ensalada Blanca

This salad combines some great flavors. It is very easy to make, and it's one of our favorites. We use grilled chicken, but you could use any leftover cooked chicken or deli roast chicken. Substitute your favorite dressing for the lime juice and salsa, if you like.

Serves 4

4 cups chopped grilled chicken

1 head iceberg lettuce, shredded

2 large tomatoes, diced

2 Hass avocados, peeled, pitted, and cut into 1-inch cubes

2 cups shredded *queso Chihuahua* or Monterey Jack cheese

¼ cup finely chopped cilantro

4 slices cooked bacon, crumbled

1 lime, quartered

1 cup Los Barrios Salsa (see page 7) or your favorite
store-bought brand

1. Combine the chicken, lettuce, tomatoes, avocados, cheese, cilantro, and bacon in a large bowl and toss to mix well.

2. Arrange the salad on individual plates, and squeeze the juice from 1 lime quarter over each serving. Drizzle the salsa over the top or serve on the side.

MANGO SALAD

Like my mother before me, I wanted to learn to make all of my husband's favorite dishes. This refreshing salad was one of the first I tried. It is his absolute favorite salad, and now it is my sons' favorite salad, too. When I recently made it for an Easter dinner, I decorated the mold with edible flowers—it looked gorgeous.

Serves 10 to 12

> Two 3-ounce packages lemon Jell-O
> 2 cups boiling water
> 6 ounces cream cheese, at room temperature
> Juice of 1 lemon
> 2 cups canned mangoes in syrup

1. Put the Jell-O in a blender, add the boiling water, and blend for 10 seconds (see Note). Add the cream cheese and lemon juice and blend until thoroughly mixed. Add the mangoes, with their syrup, and blend until pureed.

2. Pour the mixture into an 8 by 8-inch glass baking dish or 1-quart mold, cover, and refrigerate overnight, or until set.

N O T E : You will have to blend the mixture in two batches. I use a large pitcher to hold the first batch after it's blended, then pour both batches into the mold.

RED, GREEN, AND YELLOW PEPPER SALAD

Serves 4 to 6

3 tablespoons olive oil

2 garlic cloves, finely chopped

1 red bell pepper, cut into thin strips

1 yellow bell pepper, cut into thin strips

1 green bell pepper, cut into thin strips

1 teaspoon dried oregano

Salt and pepper to taste

1. Heat the olive oil in a large skillet over medium heat. Add the garlic and cook just until lightly colored, about 1 minute.

2. Add the peppers and cook, stirring, until softened, about 2 minutes. Season with the oregano and salt and pepper.

3. Serve hot, at room temperature, or chilled.

This salad is great with meat dishes. I like to serve the cold version as a side dish when I'm giving a party. You could also make the salad with roasted peppers (see page 79).

SAN ANTONIO CHICKEN SALAD

Serves 4

4 cups shredded cooked chicken

4 cups torn lettuce leaves, such as romaine, radicchio,
and other mixed greens

2 Red Delicious apples, peeled, cored, and chopped

One 10-ounce can artichoke hearts, drained and chopped

One 15-ounce can red kidney beans, drained

½ cup store-bought spicy or hot peanuts

¼ red onion, thinly sliced

2 tablespoons finely chopped cilantro

1 cup shredded *queso Chihuahua* or Monterey Jack cheese

½ cup prepared ranch dressing

½ cup prepared barbecue sauce

1. Combine all the ingredients except the dressing and barbecue sauce in a large bowl and toss to mix well. Cover and refrigerate for at least 1 hour, until chilled.

2. Meanwhile, combine the ranch dressing and barbecue sauce in a small bowl. Cover and refrigerate.

3. Serve the salad with the dressing on the side.

VARIATIONS: Add or substitute other favorite ingredients, such as different nuts, dried fruits, and various cheeses.
- Substitute *queso añejo* (crumbly white Mexican cheese) or feta cheese for the *queso Chihuahua.*
- Any kind of cooked chicken can be used: broiled, roasted, grilled, or barbecued.
- Add sliced jalapeños for spiciness.

SPICY JELL-O VEGETABLE SALAD

This is a different take on Jell-O salad. You might not think these ingredients would work, but just wait until you try it. Perfect for a luncheon on a warm summer day.

Serves 8 to 10

One 3-ounce package Jell-O (lemon, lime, orange, or orange-pineapple)

¾ teaspoon salt

1 cup boiling water

¾ cup cold water

2 tablespoons white vinegar

2 teaspoons grated onion

Dash of pepper

¾ cup finely chopped cabbage

1 green bell pepper, finely chopped

2 tablespoons diced pimiento

1 tablespoon chopped jalapeño *chile*

1. Put the Jell-O and salt in a large bowl, add the boiling water, and stir until dissolved. Add the cold water, vinegar, onion, and pepper. Cover and refrigerate for 1 to 1½ hours, until thickened but not set.

2. Fold the vegetables, pimiento, and *chile* into the Jell-O mixture. Pour into a 1-quart mold. Cover and refrigerate for 6 hours, or until set.

ENTRÉES

Arroz con Pollo 89

Beef Stew Zuazua-Style 90

Best Tex-Mex Enchiladas 93

Cactus with Eggs and Chile Sauce 94

Carne Guisada 96

Chalupa "Sandwiches" with Sour Cream 98

Chalupas Especiales 99

Chalupas Mariachi 100

Chalupas Mexicanas 101

Chalupas Vallarta 102

Chicken a la Viola 103

Chicken Breasts in Creamy

Poblano Sauce 105

Chicken Chipotle 106

Chicken in Cilantro Sauce 107

Chicken in Tangy Tomato Sauce 108

Chicken with Olives 109

Chicken with Summer Squash 111

Chilaquiles with Chicken 112

Chiles Rellenos 113

Chili con Carne 115

Commerce Street Steak Sandwich 116

Enchiladas Rancheras 118

Enchiladas Verdes 119

Enchiladas with Spinach 121

Flank Steak with Cheese and Tomatillo Sauce 123

Garlic Shrimp 124

Jammin' Apricot Ribs 125

Milk-Fed Goat in Tomato Sauce 126

Oxtails 128

Picadillo 129

Pork Chop Lover's Delight 130

Pork Tips in Red Chile Sauce 131

Puffy Tacos 132

Red Snapper in Garlic-Butter Sauce 134

Roland's Burgers with Herbs 135

Shrimp Quesadillas 136

Soft Rolled Beef Tacos with Tomato Sauce 138

Steak Fajitas with Citrus Marinade 139

Steak Milanesa 140

Steak Ranchero 141

Street Vendor Ham and Cheese Sandwiches 142

Tacos a la Diana 143

Tamale Pie 144

Tamales a la Mexicana 145

Tamarind Pork Loin 146

Vermicelli Noodle Soup with Meatballs 147

ARROZ CON POLLO (CHICKEN WITH RICE)

Serves 4 to 6

> ¾ cup vegetable oil
>
> One 2½- to 3-pound fryer chicken, cut into 8 to 10 pieces
>
> 2 cups white rice
>
> ½ onion, sliced
>
> ½ green bell pepper, chopped
>
> 3 tomatoes, halved and grated on the large holes
>
>   of a box grater
>
> 2 garlic cloves, crushed into a paste
>
> Salt to taste
>
> ¼ teaspoon pepper

1. Heat ¼ cup of the oil in a large heavy skillet or a Dutch oven over medium heat. Add the chicken and cook, turning occasionally, until golden brown and just cooked through, 25 to 30 minutes.

2. Meanwhile, in a large pot, heat the remaining ½ cup oil over medium heat. Add the rice and cook, stirring and tossing, until golden. Add the onion, bell pepper, tomatoes, and garlic, then season with salt and the pepper.

3. Add 4 cups of water and the chicken to the rice and bring to a simmer. Cover, reduce the heat, and simmer gently until the rice is tender and all the water is absorbed, about 15 minutes.

BEEF STEW ZUAZUA-STYLE

Cortadillo Zuazua

Zuazua is a town in the Mexican state of Nuevo León. *Cortadillo* is one of my favorites of the dishes my mother's beloved godmother, Madrina Amelia, used to make when we visited her. Similar to a stew, it is braised cubes of beef tenderloin, with lots of oregano for its distinctive flavor.

Serves 6

3 tablespoons vegetable oil

3 pounds beef tenderloin, cut into 1-inch cubes

Pinch of garlic powder

Salt and pepper to taste

3 tomatoes, chopped

½ onion, chopped

1 cup water

2 tablespoons dried oregano

1. Heat 2 tablespoons of the oil in a large deep skillet or a Dutch oven over medium heat. Season the beef with the garlic powder and salt and pepper. Add to the pan, in batches, and cook, turning occasionally, until browned on all sides, 6 to 8 minutes per batch. Drain the juices into a small bowl and set aside. Return all the meat to the pan.

2. Add the remaining 1 tablespoon oil to the pan, then add the tomatoes and onion and cook about 8 minutes. Return the reserved juices to the pan, add the water and oregano, and bring to a simmer. Reduce the heat to medium-low, and simmer for 5 minutes longer.

Serve this delicious stew with warm corn tortillas (see page 4), Spanish Rice (see page 165), Refried Beans (see page 163), and sliced avocados.

THE BEST TEX-MEX ENCHILADAS

At Los Barrios, we are very proud of all our food, but we are especially proud of our enchiladas. Whether from a local critic or a tourist from Australia, we always receive rave reviews for them. And some of our out-of-town guests like them so much, they ask us to freeze some to take back home. We prepared our first batch of frozen enchiladas in the early 1980s, and they traveled all the way to Hawaii, where one of our longtime customers had moved. Since then, he has been transferred all over, but he still manages to get "his fix." Then there is the young housewife whose husband was transferred to Phoenix. After they moved, she started sending us plastic containers to fill with frozen enchiladas! And the college student whose mother took her several dozen of our enchiladas to share with her friends—and the daughter refused to part with even one. And there is my brother Louie's fraternity brother from St. Louis, who surprised his pregnant wife on her thirtieth birthday by having the food for the party shipped from Los Barrios. All she had craved throughout her pregnancy were Los Barrios enchiladas. She was not happy at the thought of sharing them, but she agreed to once she found out that her husband had reserved a whole tray for the two of them to enjoy afterward. These enchiladas are that good, and now you can make them at home. But in case you don't want to, just call us, and we will freeze some and ship them to you!

Our cheese enchiladas are made with red corn tortillas, American cheese, our Enchilada Gravy Sauce, and chili con carne. Top them off with diced onions and more cheese, allow the cheese to melt, and you will have yourself a plate of the yummiest enchiladas! Figure on two or three per person, but they are so good, you may end up making dozens more.

BEST TEX-MEX ENCHILADAS

Dip corn tortillas, homemade (see page 4) or store-bought, into a skillet of hot oil to soften. Drain, fill with grated American cheese, and roll up. Place seam side down in a baking dish and cover with Enchilada Gravy Sauce (see page 3) and Chili con Carne (see page 115). Top with diced onion and more cheese. Place in a preheated 350°F oven and heat for 10 minutes, or until the cheese has melted. Remove from the oven and dig in!

CACTUS WITH EGGS AND CHILE SAUCE

Nopalitos

In Mexico, *nopalitos* are traditionally served as an entrée during Lent. **However, Nuevo Latino chefs are using them more often now as a side dish or in a salad.**

Serves 4 to 6

2 pounds fresh *nopalitos* (cactus leaves), dethorned and sliced,
    or two 16-ounce cans *nopalitos* (see Note)
4 ancho *chiles*
2 garlic cloves
3 tablespoons vegetable oil
½ onion, diced
½ bunch cilantro, tough stems removed, finely chopped
Salt and pepper to taste
6 eggs, beaten

1. If using fresh *nopalitos*, cook them in a saucepan of boiling salted water for 15 minutes. Drain and set aside.

2. Put the *chiles* in a small saucepan, add water to cover by 2 inches, and bring to a boil. Boil for 5 minutes, then drain and let cool slightly. Peel off the skin from the *chiles*, cut them in half, and remove the seeds. Transfer to a blender, add the garlic, and blend to a puree.

3. Heat the oil in a large skillet over medium heat. Add the onion and sauté until translucent, about 5 minutes. Add the *nopalitos* and heat through. Add the cilantro and salt and pepper to taste. Add the eggs and scramble them with the *nopalitos.* Add the *chile* puree and cook for 2 to 3 minutes longer.

NOTE: In San Antonio, many *molinos*, independent tortilla factories, sell prepared *nopalitos*. You can also find them in some Latin grocery stores.

Serve these with warm flour tortillas (see page 6), Refried Beans (see page 163), and Guacamole (see page 47). During Lent, Mexican Bread Pudding (see page 180) would be served as dessert after this meal.

CARNE GUISADA (BEEF STEW)

Serves 4 to 6

2 tablespoons vegetable oil

2 pounds boneless top sirloin, cut into 1-inch cubes

1½ teaspoons garlic powder

1 tablespoon salt

1½ teaspoons pepper

2 tomatoes, diced

2 potatoes, peeled and cut into 1-inch cubes

1 onion, chopped

1 green bell pepper, chopped

½ cup tomato sauce

1. Heat 1 tablespoon of oil in a deep skillet over medium heat. Season the meat with the garlic powder, salt, and pepper, add to the pan, cover, and cook until the meat is about three-quarters cooked, 8 to 10 minutes. Drain the meat juices into a small bowl and set aside.

2. Add the rest of the oil, tomatoes, potatoes, onion, and bell pepper to the pan with the meat and cook until the onion is lightly browned. Add the tomato sauce and the reserved meat juices and bring to a simmer, then reduce the heat to medium-low and simmer gently for 15 minutes. Serve immediately.

Serve with warm flour tortillas (see page 6).

CHALUPAS

Chalupas are like small Mexican pizzas. You start off with a corn tortilla that is deep-fried until crunchy. Usually the first layer is refried beans, then you add whatever toppings you desire, from chorizo (Mexican sausage) to chicken to guacamole and sour cream. The combinations are endless. Try our different chalupas, then try your own variations. You will be amazed at all the versions you come up with.

Chalupa shells can be found in Latin groceries, or you can make them at home by frying corn tortillas, homemade (see page 4) or store-bought, in hot oil for a few seconds.

CHALUPA "SANDWICHES" WITH SOUR CREAM

Chalupas con Crema

Serves 4

> 2 cups Guacamole (see page 47)
> 8 chalupa shells
> 2 cups shredded cooked chicken
> 1 cup sour cream

1. Spread ½ cup of the guacamole over one of the chalupa shells. Layer ½ cup of the chicken over it. Spread ¼ cup of the sour cream over another shell and place, sour cream side down, over the chicken to make a sandwich.

2. Repeat with the remaining ingredients to make a total of four sandwiches.

3. Serve with a fresh tomato salad on the side, if you like.

CHALUPAS ESPECIALES

Serves 4

8 chalupa shells

1 cup Guacamole (see page 47)

2 cups shredded cooked chicken

1 cup sour cream

1 cup crumbled *queso añejo* (crumbly white
Mexican cheese) or feta cheese

1. Preheat the oven to 325°F.

2. Place the chalupa shells on a cookie sheet and put in the oven for 3 to 4 minutes, until heated through.

3. Spread 2 tablespoons of the guacamole on each chalupa shell. Cover with the chicken. Top with the sour cream, sprinkle with the cheese, and serve immediately.

CHALUPAS MARIACHI

Serves 4

1½ cups refried beans, homemade (see page 163) or
    store-bought
8 chalupa shells
2 cups shredded American cheese
2 Hass avocados, peeled, pitted, and sliced
Chopped jalapeño *chiles* for garnish

1. Preheat the oven to 325°F.

2. Heat the beans in a small saucepan over medium heat. Spread the beans evenly over the chalupa shells. Top with the cheese.

3. Place the chalupas on a cookie sheet and put in the oven for 1 to 2 minutes, or until the cheese has melted. Top the chalupas with the avocados, garnish with the *chiles*, and serve.

CHALUPAS MEXICANAS

Serves 4

¼ pound chorizo (Mexican sausage), casings removed

¼ onion, chopped

1 to 2 serrano *chiles,* finely chopped

1 tomato, diced

1 cup refried beans, homemade (see page 163) or
   store-bought

8 chalupa shells

4 cups shredded lettuce

1 cup crumbled *queso añejo* (crumbly white
   Mexican cheese) or your favorite cheese

1 Hass avocado, peeled, pitted, and sliced

1. Preheat the oven to 325°F.

2. Cook the sausage in a medium skillet over medium heat for about 1 minute, stirring to break up any lumps. Add the onion and sauté until softened, 2 to 3 minutes. Add the *chiles* and half of the tomato and cook until softened. Spoon off any excess fat from the pan. Stir in the beans and cook until heated through, 4 to 5 minutes.

3. Meanwhile, place the chalupa shells on a cookie sheet and put in the oven for 3 to 4 minutes, until heated through.

4. Spread the bean mixture over the chalupa shells. Top with the lettuce, the remaining tomato, and the cheese, and garnish with avocado slices.

CHALUPAS VALLARTA

These chalupas make an especially pretty presentation. I like to think of them as "garden chalupas."

Serves 4

8 chalupa shells

2 cups refried beans, homemade (see page 163) or
    store-bought

2 cups shredded cooked chicken

2 cups shredded lettuce

2 tomatoes, diced

1 cup Guacamole (see page 47)

¼ carrot, peeled and shredded

1 onion, sliced into rings

1 cup grated American cheese or your favorite cheese

¾ cup sour cream

1. Preheat the oven to 325°F.

2. Place the chalupa shells on a cookie sheet and put in the oven for 3 to 4 minutes, until heated through.

3. Meanwhile, heat the beans in a small saucepan over low heat.

4. Spread the beans over the chalupa shells. Top with the chicken, then the lettuce, tomato, and guacamole. Garnish with the carrot and top each chalupa with an onion ring. Sprinkle the cheese over the top, and garnish each one with a dollop of sour cream.

CHICKEN A LA VIOLA

When we were growing up, my mother would make this for a special Sunday night dinner, or when we were having guests. She talked about watching her grandmother make this dish when she was a little girl. The recipe had never been written down, but my mother re-created it from memory. We serve this at the restaurant today, and it makes me feel good every time I see a plate of it going by. It feels as if company has just arrived.

Serves 8 to 12

Two 2½- to 3-pound fryer chickens, cut into 8 pieces each

2 tablespoons salt

8 tomatoes

8 garlic cloves

2 tablespoons olive oil

1 onion, thinly sliced

1 green bell pepper, sliced lengthwise into strips

2 tablespoons dried oregano

½ teaspoon ground cumin

Salt and pepper to taste

1. Sprinkle the chicken with the salt. Place all of the chicken in a large pot, cover, and cook over medium heat for 30 minutes, turning it often (be careful to avoid the hot steam when you remove the lid). Remove the chicken from heat and set aside. Reserve the juices from the pot.

2. Meanwhile, bring a large pot of water to a boil. Add the tomatoes and garlic and cook until they are very soft, 10 to 12 minutes. Using tongs or a slotted spoon, remove the tomatoes and let cool slightly. (Discard garlic and cooking water.) Peel off the skins, put the tomatoes in a bowl, and, using a potato masher, mash to a puree.

3. Heat the oil in a large stockpot over medium heat. In batches, add the chicken and brown lightly on both sides, about 8 minutes per side. Return all the chicken to the pot. Add the onion and bell pepper to the pot and cook for 3 to 4 minutes until tender. Add the oregano and cumin and season with salt and pepper, then add the pureed tomatoes and the reserved chicken juices, bring to a simmer, and cook for 10 minutes. Serve hot.

Serve this with Mexican Rice (see page 159), Refried Beans (see page 163), and warm corn tortillas (see page 4).

CHICKEN BREASTS IN CREAMY POBLANO SAUCE

Serves 8

1 tablespoon salt, plus more to taste

8 skinless, boneless chicken breasts

One 8-ounce package cream cheese, at room temperature

2 poblano *chiles,* roasted (see page 79), peeled, and seeded

One 15-ounce can chicken broth

4 tablespoons (½ stick) butter

Salt and pepper to taste

1. Fill a large pot with 4 quarts water, add the 1 tablespoon salt and the chicken, and bring to a boil. Boil gently for 20 minutes. Drain the chicken thoroughly.

2. Meanwhile, preheat the oven to 300°F. Grease a 9 by 13-inch baking dish.

3. Combine the cream cheese, *chiles,* chicken broth, and butter in a blender, and blend until smooth and creamy. Season with salt and pepper, and blend well.

4. Place the chicken in the prepared baking dish. Pour the sauce over the chicken and bake for 20 minutes.

Serve this chicken with Spanish Rice (see page 165).

CHICKEN CHIPOTLE

Chipotle *chiles* can be very hot. When making the sauce, you may want to start with 1 or 2 *chiles*, then taste the sauce and add more chipotles if desired.

Serves 4

4 skinless, boneless chicken breasts

½ cup chopped onion

2 garlic cloves

1 tablespoon salt

One 8-ounce package cream cheese, at room temperature

1 cup milk

4 canned chipotle *chiles*

Salt and pepper to taste

⅛ teaspoon paprika

1. Place the chicken breasts, onion, garlic cloves, and 1 tablespoon of salt in a large pot and add water to cover. Bring to a boil and cook for 20 minutes. Drain well.

2. Meanwhile, preheat the oven to 325°F. Grease a 9 by 13-inch baking dish.

3. Combine the cream cheese, milk, *chiles,* and salt and pepper in a blender and blend well.

4. Place the chicken in the prepared baking dish. Pour the sauce over the chicken and sprinkle with the paprika. Bake for 20 minutes.

Serve this chicken with Mexican Rice (see page 159) and Charro-Style Beans (see page 151), along with corn tortillas (see page 4). I often heat the tortillas over an open flame, allowing them to burn a little at the edges.

CHICKEN IN CILANTRO SAUCE

Pollo al Cilantro

This makes a delightful brunch or lunch dish. It's very easy to prepare, and it will wow your guests.

Serves 6

6 skinless, boneless chicken breasts

1 bunch cilantro, tough stems removed, finely chopped

2 to 3 serrano *chiles* (to taste)

One 10-ounce can evaporated milk

Salt and pepper to taste

2 tablespoons vegetable oil

¼ onion, sliced

1. Place the chicken breasts in a large pot, add water to cover, and bring to a boil. Reduce the heat and cook for 30 minutes. Drain thoroughly. Transfer to a serving platter and cover to keep warm.

2. Meanwhile, combine the cilantro, *chiles*, milk, and salt and pepper in a blender and blend thoroughly, 2 to 3 minutes.

3. Heat the oil in a medium saucepan over medium heat. Sauté the onion until translucent, 3 to 4 minutes. Add the cilantro mixture and bring to a simmer. Reduce the heat to low and simmer gently for 10 minutes.

4. Pour the sauce over the chicken and serve.

Serve this chicken with our delicious Spanish Rice (see page 165).

CHICKEN IN TANGY TOMATO SAUCE

Pollo en Salsa

Serves 4 to 6

2 tablespoons vegetable oil

One 2½- to 3-pound fryer chicken, cut into 8 to 10 pieces

2 tablespoons garlic salt

1 tablespoon dried oregano

Pepper to taste

1 onion, cut in half and sliced

1 green bell pepper, cut into strips

2 celery stalks, chopped

One 8-ounce can tomato sauce

3 tablespoons prepared mustard

2 cups water

---

1. Heat the oil in a 4-quart Dutch oven over medium heat. Season the chicken with the garlic salt, oregano, and pepper. Add the chicken to the pot, increase the heat to medium-high, and cook, turning occasionally, until browned on all sides, about 20 minutes.

---

2. Scatter the onion, bell pepper, and celery over the chicken. Combine the tomato sauce, mustard, and water in a small bowl, mixing well. Pour this mixture over the chicken, reduce the heat to low, and cook for 30 minutes longer.

---

3. Serve the chicken on a bed of Spanish Rice (see page 165) with the sauce spooned over the top.

CHICKEN WITH OLIVES

Cazuela de Pollo con Aceitunas

Serves 4 to 6

1 tablespoon olive oil

4 chicken drumsticks

4 chicken thighs

Salt and pepper to taste

1 onion, diced

2 garlic cloves, finely chopped

1 bay leaf

1 teaspoon ground cumin

½ teaspoon dried thyme

½ cup chopped pitted green olives

½ cup chopped pitted black olives

¾ cup dry white wine

¾ cup chicken broth

1½ teaspoons cornstarch, dissolved in 1 tablespoon
cold water

1. Heat the oil in a large deep skillet over medium-high heat. Season the chicken with salt and pepper. Add the chicken to the pan and cook, turning occasionally, until browned on all sides, about 20 minutes. Remove the chicken from the pan and set aside.

2. Add the onion to the pan, reduce the heat to medium, and sauté until soft, about 3 minutes. Add the garlic, bay leaf, cumin, and thyme and cook, stirring, for 1 minute. Return the chicken to the pan, add the olives and wine, cover, and cook for 20 to 25 minutes, until the chicken is cooked through. Transfer the chicken to a serving platter and cover to keep warm.

3. Continue to simmer the sauce until the liquid is reduced by half. Add the broth, raise the heat, and bring to a boil. Stir in the cornstarch mixture, reduce the heat, and cook, stirring constantly, until the sauce thickens. Pour the sauce over the chicken and serve immediately.

Serve the chicken on a bed of white rice, with steamed zucchini and garlic bread.

CHICKEN WITH SUMMER SQUASH

Pollo con Calabacita

When you prepare this dish, it fills the house with such delicious aromas that your neighbors will surely come running over.

Serves 4 to 6

¼ cup vegetable oil

One 2½- to 3-pound fryer chicken, cut into 8 to 10 pieces

1 teaspoon salt, plus more to taste

4 tatuma squash (zucchini or summer squash can be substituted),
   halved, seeded, and cut into 1-inch cubes (see Note)

4 tomatoes, cut in half and sliced

½ onion, sliced

2 garlic cloves, finely chopped

4 to 5 whole serrano *chiles* (to taste) (optional)

1½ teaspoons to 1 tablespoon dried oregano (to taste)

½ teaspoon pepper

1. Heat the oil in a large skillet over medium heat. Season the chicken with the 1 teaspoon salt, add to the pan, and cook, turning once or twice, until golden brown, about 15 minutes. Pour off the excess fat.

2. Add the squash, tomatoes, onion, garlic, *chiles,* if using, and oregano. Season with salt (the chicken has already been salted, so be careful not to oversalt the dish), and the pepper. Cover and simmer until the chicken is cooked through and the squash is fork-tender, 10 to 15 minutes. Transfer to a serving platter, and enjoy.

NOTE: If using zucchini or summer squash, which cook faster than tatuma, add to the pan 5 minutes before the chicken is done.

CHILAQUILES WITH CHICKEN

Assemble this casserole right before baking; if it is prepared ahead of time, the sauce may make the tortilla strips soggy.

Serves 8

2 cups fried tortilla strips (see Note)

4 cups shredded cooked chicken

1½ cups Green Tomatillo Sauce (see page 119)

1 cup shredded *queso Chihuahua* or Monterey Jack cheese

1 cup sour cream

1. Preheat the oven to 350°F.

2. Spread the tortilla strips over the bottom of a 9 by 13-inch baking dish. Place the chicken on top and cover with the sauce. Scatter the cheese over the top. Cover with foil and bake for 20 minutes, or until heated through.

3. Spread the sour cream over the top of the casserole, and serve.

N O T E : To make fried tortilla strips, slice corn tortillas, homemade (see page 4) or store-bought, into thin strips. Fry in a large skillet of hot oil until light golden brown and crisp; watch carefully so they do not burn. Remove with a slotted spoon and drain on paper towels.

CHILES RELLENOS ☀

*C*hiles rellenos means stuffed peppers. They can be stuffed with almost anything you like; some popular fillings are *queso añejo* (crumbly white Mexican cheese), chicken, and even cooked diced vegetables. Some recipes add nuts and raisins to the meat filling.

Serves 8

¼ cup olive oil

2 pounds ground beef or chopped brisket

½ teaspoon salt

½ teaspoon pepper

½ teaspoon garlic powder

½ teaspoon ground cumin

1 potato, peeled and diced

1 carrot, peeled and diced

8 roasted poblano *chiles* (see page 79)

5 eggs, separated, yolks beaten

Vegetable oil for frying

Flour for coating

Warm Mild Tomato Sauce (see page 13) (optional)

1. Heat the olive oil in a large skillet over medium heat. Add the beef, season with the salt, pepper, garlic powder, and cumin, and cook, stirring to break up any lumps, until browned, 6 to 8 minutes. Add the potato and carrot and cook, stirring occasionally, until fork-tender, 8 to 10 minutes. Remove from the heat.

2. After peeling off the skins from the poblanos, make a slit down the side of each *chile*, and remove the seeds. Stuff the *chiles* with the meat mixture, dividing it evenly.

3. In a large bowl, beat the egg whites until they form stiff peaks. Beat in the egg yolks.

4. Pour 1 inch of vegetable oil into a large deep skillet and heat until very hot. Spread the flour on a sheet of waxed paper. When the oil is hot, one at a time, roll the stuffed peppers in the flour to coat, then dip into the egg batter and add to the pan. Cook one at a time until lightly browned on the bottom, 30 to 60 seconds. Turn and cook until browned on the second side. Remove with a slotted spoon and drain briefly on paper towels.

5. Place the *chiles* on a serving platter and top with the sauce, if desired.

CHILI CON CARNE

When the leaves start to change color and the first cold front moves in, everyone is ready for that big bowl of chili. Here is the recipe to satisfy that yearning.

Serves 4

1 pound ground beef

1 teaspoon garlic powder

1 teaspoon ground cumin

1 bay leaf

Salt and pepper to taste

2 tablespoons chili powder

1 cup water

2 cups cooked or canned pinto beans (optional)

1 cup shredded American or Cheddar cheese

½ cup chopped onion

1. Brown the beef in a large skillet over medium heat. Add the garlic powder, cumin, and bay leaf, and season with salt and pepper. Cook, stirring occasionally, for 15 minutes (add a little water if the pan becomes dry).

2. Add the chili powder and water, stirring well, and bring to a simmer. Simmer for 10 minutes. Add the beans, if using, and heat through.

3. Remove the bay leaf and spoon the chili into bowls. Garnish with the cheese and onion.

Serve with warm flour tortillas (see page 6) or crackers.

COMMERCE STREET STEAK SANDWICH

When my parents were dating, they had lunch almost every day at a small diner on Commerce Street. This recipe comes from that diner, and my mother says it was one of my father's favorites. It may become one of your favorites as well.

Makes 6 sandwiches

BLACK BEAN MAYONNAISE

1¼ cups mayonnaise

One 16-ounce can black beans, drained and chopped

SANDWICHES

Six 6-ounce thinly sliced flank steaks

Salt and pepper to taste

1 tablespoon garlic powder

6 *bolillos* (small, elongated hard rolls) or 6-inch French breads

1 tablespoon olive oil

Garlic powder to taste

12 slices *queso Chihuahua* or Monterey Jack cheese

6 tomato slices, cut in half

6 red-leaf lettuce leaves

---

1. To make the black bean mayonnaise, combine the mayonnaise and chopped beans in a small bowl, stirring until thoroughly blended. Cover and refrigerate until needed.

---

2. Season the steaks with salt, pepper, and garlic powder. Cook steaks separately in a heated skillet over medium-high heat for 4 to 5 minutes on each side. Remove from pan and set aside.

---

3. To make the sandwiches, split the *bolillos* in half. Brush the cut sides with the olive oil and sprinkle with the garlic powder. Toast cut side down on a stovetop grill or in a large skillet.

---

4. Spread the mayonnaise over the cut sides of the rolls and top with the cheese. Place cut side up on the grill, or in the oven (preheated to 350°F), until the cheese has melted. Add the beef and season with salt and pepper. Garnish with the tomatoes and lettuce, and serve.

VARIATION: You can also make these by spreading a *chimichurri* sauce, available in Latin markets, or pesto on the bread before toasting, instead of the olive oil and garlic powder.

ENCHILADAS RANCHERAS

This is one of the most requested dishes on our menu. Feel free to steam the tortillas instead of frying them. You could also fill them with cheese only, omitting the chicken. Either way, they are very tasty.

Serves 4

Vegetable oil for frying

12 corn tortillas, homemade (see page 4) or
    store-bought

1½ cups shredded cooked chicken

2 cups Salsa Ranchera (see page 10)

¾ cup sour cream

1½ cups crumbled *queso fresco* (crumbly white
    Mexican cheese) or feta cheese

1. Pour ½ inch of vegetable oil into a large skillet and heat over medium-high heat until hot. One at a time, dip the tortillas into the hot oil to soften them, just a few seconds. Transfer to paper towels to drain.

2. Fill the center of the tortillas with the chicken and roll up. Place seam side down on individual plates and top with the sauce and sour cream. Sprinkle the cheese over the top.

Serve the enchiladas with Spanish Rice (see page 165), Refried Beans (see page 163), and Guacamole (see page 47).

ENCHILADAS VERDES

The tomatillo sauce for these enchiladas can be quite tangy, depending on the tomatillos. This is one of the most popular dishes at our restaurant.

Serves 6

GREEN TOMATILLO SAUCE

1 pound tomatillos

2 garlic cloves

2 tablespoons vegetable oil

½ onion, finely chopped

Salt and pepper to taste

ENCHILADAS

Vegetable oil for frying

12 corn tortillas, homemade (see page 4) or store-bought

2 cups shredded cooked chicken or shredded *queso*
　　　Chihuahua or Monterey Jack cheese

¾ cup sour cream

Chopped cilantro

1. To make the sauce, soak the tomatillos in a bowl of cold water to loosen the husks. Drain, and peel off the husks.

2. Place the tomatillos and garlic in a saucepan with water to cover the tomatillos halfway and bring to a boil. Boil until the tomatillos are soft, about 10 minutes. Drain. Transfer the tomatillos and garlic to a blender and blend to a puree.

3. Heat the 2 tablespoons oil in a medium saucepan over medium heat. Add the pureed tomatillos and the onion, and season with salt and pepper. Bring to a simmer, and simmer for about 5 minutes.

4. Meanwhile, pour ½ inch of vegetable oil into a large skillet and heat over medium-high heat until hot. One at a time, dip the tortillas into the hot oil to soften them, just a few seconds. Transfer to paper towels to drain.

5. Fill the center of the tortillas with the chicken or cheese and fold over the sides. Place seam side down on individual plates and top with the warm sauce. Garnish with the sour cream, and enjoy.

VARIATION: You can also use this sauce as a dipping sauce for tortilla chips or as a salsa in other dishes: Add 1 serrano *chile,* finely chopped, and 1 to 2 tablespoons chopped cilantro, to taste.

ENCHILADAS WITH SPINACH

These spinach enchiladas are fantastic and are always a big hit when added to our menu as a daily special.

Serves 4 to 6

ENCHILADAS

¼ cup olive oil

12 corn tortillas, homemade (see page 4) or store-bought

1½ cups shredded *queso Chihuahua* or Monterey Jack cheese

1½ cups shredded Cheddar cheese

1 onion, chopped

2 cups diced cooked chicken

SAUCE

One 10-ounce box chopped frozen spinach, cooked and drained

1 cup chicken broth

2 scallions, chopped

½ cup fresh green *chiles*

1 cup sour cream

1. Preheat the oven to 350°F.

2. Heat the oil in a large skillet over medium-high heat until hot. One at a time, dip the tortillas into the hot oil to soften them, just a few seconds. Transfer to paper towels to drain.

3. Combine the cheeses in a bowl, tossing to mix well. Reserve ½ cup of the cheese in a small bowl. Fill the center of the tortillas with the remaining 2½ cups cheese, the onion, and the chicken. Roll up and place seam side down in a baking dish.

4. To make the sauce, combine the spinach, chicken broth, scallions, *chiles,* and sour cream in a blender and blend thoroughly. Pour the sauce over the enchiladas. Scatter the reserved cheese over the top. Cover and bake for 30 minutes, or until the sauce is bubbly.

VARIATION: Omit the chicken. Melt ¼ pound (1 stick) butter in a large skillet. Add 2 cups precooked baby shrimp, 2 garlic cloves, finely chopped, and ½ cup lemon juice and cook, stirring, until the garlic is softened, 2 to 3 minutes. Fill the enchiladas as directed, substituting the shrimp for the chicken.

FLANK STEAK WITH CHEESE AND TOMATILLO SAUCE

Sábanas de Res

Serves 4

> 2 tablespoons vegetable oil
>
> Four 6-ounce flank steaks, pounded until thin
>
> Garlic powder to taste
>
> Salt and pepper to taste
>
> 1 cup refried beans, homemade (see page 163) or
>   store-bought, warmed
>
> 1 cup Green Tomatillo Sauce (see page 119)
>
> 1 cup shredded asadero or mozzarella cheese

1. Preheat the broiler.

2. Heat a large skillet over medium-high heat until hot, then add the oil. Season the steaks with garlic powder and salt and pepper. Add to the pan and cook, turning once, for 5 to 6 minutes on each side. Transfer the steaks to four broilerproof serving plates.

3. Spread a thin layer of beans over each steak, cover with the sauce, and sprinkle with the cheese. Place under the broiler just until the cheese is melted.

GARLIC SHRIMP

Camarones al Ajillo

Serves 6

½ cup olive oil

1 onion, diced

2 garlic cloves, finely chopped

1 guajillo *chile,* thinly sliced

Salt and pepper to taste

2 pounds extra-large shrimp, peeled and deveined

1. Heat the oil in a large saucepan over medium heat. Add the onion and garlic and cook until the onion is translucent and the garlic is just golden. Add the *chile,* and salt and pepper, and cook until tender, about 5 minutes.

2. Add the shrimp and cook, stirring constantly, until pink and opaque throughout, about 5 minutes. Serve with white rice.

JAMMIN' APRICOT RIBS

Costillas con Mermelada

Serves 4

6 pounds beef short ribs

Garlic powder to taste

Salt and pepper to taste

½ cup apricot preserves

½ cup Los Barrios Salsa (see page 7) or your favorite

    store-bought brand

½ cup water

1. Preheat the oven to 325°F.

2. Season the ribs with garlic powder and salt and pepper. Place in a roasting pan and spread the preserves over the ribs. Pour the salsa over the ribs, and add the water to the pan. Cover with foil and bake for 2½ hours.

3. Remove the foil and increase the oven temperature to 350°F. Bake for 30 minutes longer.

Serve these with Mexican Rice (see page 159).

MILK-FED GOAT IN TOMATO SAUCE

Cabrito en Salsa

In northern Mexico, it is a tradition when celebrating a special occasion to serve *cabrito en salsa.* When it is prepared correctly, the meat is falling-off-the-bone tender.

Serves 8 to 10

10 to 12 pounds whole milk-fed baby goat (have your
    butcher cut it into 2-inch pieces, including the bones)
½ onion, sliced
2 garlic cloves
2 bay leaves
1 tablespoon salt
½ teaspoon pepper
½ teaspoon ground cumin
1½ tablespoons chopped fresh oregano, or ½ teaspoon dried
½ cup white vinegar
3 quarts water
1 to 2 tablespoons vegetable oil (optional)
2½ cups Salsa Ranchera (see page 10) or Warm Mild
    Tomato Sauce (see page 13)

1. Place the meat in a large Dutch oven, add the onion, garlic, bay leaves, salt, pepper, cumin, oregano, vinegar, and water, and bring to a simmer. Reduce the heat to low and simmer gently until the meat is very tender, about 2½ hours. Remove from the heat. Strain the meat and set aside. Return juices to the pot. Discard solids.

2. To brown the meat, heat the oil in a large skillet. Add the meat and cook, turning occasionally, until browned on all sides. Return the meat to the pot containing the juices.

LOS BARRIOS FAMILY COOKBOOK

3. Place ¼ cup of salsa on each dinner plate. Ladle the meat on top and serve immediately.

Serve this with Refried Beans (see page 163).

OXTAILS

Whether you eat this dish with the tomatoes, or as a soup (see Variation below), you won't be disappointed! Licking your fingers may be bad manners, but with these oxtails, you won't be able to help yourself.

Serves 6 to 8

4 pounds oxtails, cut into 2-inch pieces

½ onion, cut in half, plus 1 onion, chopped

1½ teaspoons salt, plus more to taste

1 tablespoon vegetable oil

4 serrano *chiles,* sliced

4 tomatoes, chopped

1. Put the oxtails in a large pot and add water to cover. Add the onion quarters and the 1½ teaspoons salt. Bring to a simmer, reduce the heat to low, and cook for 2 hours. Remove the oxtails from the broth and set aside; spoon 3 tablespoons of the broth into a small cup. Reserve the remaining broth to serve as soup (see below), if desired.

2. Heat the oil in a large skillet over medium heat. Add the chopped onion, the *chiles,* and the tomatoes and cook until the onion is softened, 3 to 4 minutes. Add the oxtails and the 3 tablespoons reserved broth, and season with salt. Reduce the heat to low and cook until heated through, about 8 minutes. Serve hot.

VARIATION: For a delicious consommé, add ½ teaspoon dried oregano, crumbled, to the broth, and serve hot.

PICADILLO

Serve this on its own, or use it for chalupas (see pages 99 to 102), tacos (see pages 23, 24, 132, 138, and 143), or nachos (see pages 51 and 53).

Serves 6 to 8

2 pounds ground beef

3 cups warm water

½ teaspoon ground cumin

¼ teaspoon garlic powder

1 tablespoon salt

¼ teaspoon pepper

1 onion, diced

2 tomatoes, diced

1 green bell pepper, diced

1. Cook the meat in a large skillet over medium heat, stirring to break up any lumps. Cook for 7 to 8 minutes until browned. Drain off any fat. Stir in 1 cup of the water, the cumin, garlic powder, salt, and pepper and cook for 8 to 10 minutes.

2. Add the onion, tomatoes, and bell pepper and cook until the vegetables are tender, about 10 minutes. Stir in the remaining 2 cups water and simmer for 8 minutes.

VARIATION: To make this really interesting, add some pecans and raisins to the *picadillo* 2 minutes before it's done. This variation makes a great stuffing for Chiles Rellenos (see page 113).

Serve this with Mexican Rice (see page 159).

PORK CHOP LOVER'S DELIGHT

Serves 5

> 1 egg
> ½ cup milk
> 2 tablespoons all-purpose flour
> 2 cups finely crushed saltines
> Ten 4-ounce pork chops
> Salt and pepper to taste
> ½ cup vegetable oil
> 2 cups Salsa Ranchera (see page 10) or Warm Mild Tomato Sauce
> (see page 13)

1. Whisk together the egg and milk in a shallow bowl. Put the flour on a plate and spread the crushed saltines on another plate. Season the pork chops with salt and pepper. *Lightly* dredge the pork chops in the flour. Dip the pork chops in the egg mixture, then coat thoroughly with the crushed saltines.

2. Heat the oil in a large skillet over medium heat. Add the pork chops in batches and cook, turning once, until cooked through, 4 to 5 minutes per side; be careful not to let the breading burn.

3. Meanwhile, heat the sauce in a small saucepan over low heat.

4. Transfer the pork chops to individual serving plates and top with the sauce.

To crush saltines, put the crackers on a large sheet of waxed paper and roll over them with a rolling pin.

PORK TIPS IN RED CHILE SAUCE

Asado de Puerco

For as long as I can remember, this has been one of my mother's favorite dishes. There are not many things she will drop everything for (both to prepare and eat), but this is one of them. This, and her grandchildren, of course!

Serves 6

6 ancho *chiles*

2 cascabel *chiles*

10 garlic cloves, chopped

1 teaspoon dried oregano

1 teaspoon ground cumin

2 teaspoons salt

½ teaspoon pepper

½ cup olive oil (or pork fat)

3 pounds boneless pork roast, cut into bite-sized chunks

1½ cups water

1 bay leaf

1. Put the *chiles* in a small saucepan, add water to cover, and bring to a boil. Boil until the *chiles* are softened. Drain and let cool briefly, then peel off the skins and remove the seeds. Transfer the *chiles* to a blender, add the garlic, and blend until smooth. Add the oregano, cumin, salt, and pepper and blend to mix.

2. Heat the oil in a large deep skillet over medium-high heat. Add the pork and cook, stirring frequently, until browned on all sides, 15 to 20 minutes. Add the water and cook until the meat is tender and the liquid has evaporated, about 10 minutes longer.

3. Pour off the excess fat from the pan. Add the *chile* puree and bay leaf, reduce the heat to low, and simmer for 20 minutes. Remove the bay leaf before serving.

Wh)hen the Food Network came to town to film a segment for *Food Nation with Bobby Flay,* Los Barrios was ready to teach them a little about Tex-Mex. During the show, we prepared several dishes, including our puffy tacos. Of all the dishes Bobby encountered during his stay in San Antonio, these were what caught his attention. The light, fluffy tacos impressed him so much, he talked about adding them to the menu at Mesa Grill, his famed Manhattan eatery. How about that—Los Barrios hits New York!

Makes 12 to 15 tacos

3 cups corn *masa* mix (see Note)

1½ teaspoons salt

2¼ cups warm water

Vegetable oil for frying

1. Combine the *masa* mix, salt, and warm water in a large bowl and mix until a smooth dough forms. Pull off pieces of dough and roll them into balls about the size of a Ping-Pong ball.

2. Cut a quart-size resealable plastic bag open down both sides, to form a rectangle. Use the bag to line a tortilla press as you shape the tortillas, so they do not stick: Lay one side of the plastic over the bottom of the press, place a ball of dough in the center, and fold the other side of the plastic over the dough. Shut the top of the tortilla press firmly down on the dough to shape the tortilla. (See Note.)

3. Meanwhile, pour 2 inches of vegetable oil into a large deep pot and heat to 250°F.

4. Drop a tortilla into the hot oil and, using a metal spatula, repeatedly douse the tortilla with the hot oil until it begins to puff up. Flip it over and, using the spatula, make an indentation in the center of the tortilla to form a taco shape. Transfer to paper towels to drain. Repeat with the remaining tortillas. *(Caution: Be very careful when making these. Make sure there is proper ventilation, and do not allow the oil to get too hot.)*

NOTE: If you can't get your hands on a tortilla press, a clean countertop will do. You will still need the plastic so that the dough does not stick to the counter. Place a dough ball on one side of the plastic, cover with the other side, and use a heavy skillet to press out the tortilla.

Masa mix can be found at Latin markets and some larger supermarkets.

Fill each taco with 2 tablespoons of cooked ground meat or shredded chicken, Guacamole (see page 47), beans, and cheese, or your favorite filling. Top with shredded lettuce and diced tomatoes. You are in for the treat of a lifetime.

RED SNAPPER IN GARLIC-BUTTER SAUCE

You can never have too much garlic, right? Just ask Emeril. He will probably tell you that not only does it taste terrific, but it's also very good for you. Try this easy recipe and see how good it can be.

Serves 4

½ pound (2 sticks) butter

1 cup finely chopped garlic (3 to 4 heads)

2 tablespoons olive oil

1 lemon, quartered

Four 10-ounce red snapper fillets

Salt and pepper to taste

1 cup all-purpose flour

1. Melt the butter in a large saucepan. Add the garlic and cook for 3 to 4 minutes, until softened. Keep warm over very low heat.

2. Heat 1 tablespoon of the oil in a large skillet over medium heat. Squeeze the juice of the lemon over both sides of the fish fillets and season with salt and pepper. Spread the flour on a plate and lightly dredge 2 fillets in the flour, coating both sides. Place the fillets in the skillet and cook, turning once, until just cooked through, 4 to 5 minutes per side. Transfer to a platter and cover to keep warm. Repeat with the remaining fillets, adding the remaining 1 tablespoon oil to the pan.

3. Return all the fillets to the pan and pour the garlic-butter sauce over them. Simmer for 2 to 3 minutes, then serve.

Serve the fish with Spanish Rice (see page 165) and steamed vegetables.

ROLAND'S BURGERS WITH HERBS

Because we have such great weather here in the Lone Star State, we are always grilling outdoors. These burgers—named after my husband—are one of our favorite quick meals. The herbs and spices really jazz them up. If you don't feel like having hamburger buns, serve these with flour tortillas (see page 6).

Serves 6

1½ pounds ground beef
½ teaspoon garlic powder
¾ teaspoon dried oregano
¾ teaspoon ground cumin
¼ cup salsa, homemade (see pages 7 and 10)
     or store-bought

---

1. Combine all of the ingredients in a bowl and blend well. Shape into six 1-inch-thick patties.

---

2. Cook the burgers over a hot grill for 5 to 7 minutes on each side, or panfry over medium-high heat for 5 to 7 minutes on each side. Serve on buns with your favorite condiments. We like these with Refried Beans (see page 163) and sliced avocados.

SHRIMP QUESADILLAS

We serve these with rice and beans for an entrée, or on their own as an appetizer. I like to squeeze fresh lime juice over them, and add some fresh salsa. These make a great dish to take to a party (you can reheat them in the microwave for a few seconds).

Serves 4

4 tablespoons (½ stick) butter

2 garlic cloves, finely chopped

¾ pound shrimp, peeled, deveined, and cooked

12 corn tortillas, homemade (see page 4) or store-bought

1 tomato, diced

½ cup chopped cilantro

2 tablespoons finely chopped serrano *chile*

1½ cups shredded *queso Chihuahua* or Monterey Jack cheese

1. Melt the butter in a large skillet over medium heat. Add the garlic and cook until fragrant, about 2 minutes. Add the shrimp and sauté for 2 to 3 minutes. Remove from the heat.

2. Meanwhile, heat the tortillas in a steamer. Alternatively, moisten the tortillas with water and heat in a large skillet, about 30 seconds on each side, or wrap the wet tortillas in a paper towel and heat in the microwave, 15 to 20 seconds.

3. Place about 2 tablespoons shrimp in the center of a tortilla and top with 1 teaspoon diced tomato, a sprinkling of cilantro, and a little of the chopped *chile* to taste. Top with a heaping tablespoon of cheese and fold the tortilla over into a half-moon shape. Repeat to make the remaining quesadillas.

4. Heat a large skillet or a stovetop grill until hot. Add one or two of the quesadillas and cook over medium heat for 2 to 3 minutes. Flip and cook until the cheese is completely melted,

another minute or so; do not let the skillet get too hot, or the tortillas will become tough. Transfer to a platter and cover to keep warm. Repeat with the remaining quesadillas.

Serve these with Guacamole (see page 47) and Los Barrios Salsa (see page 7).

SOFT ROLLED BEEF TACOS WITH TOMATO SAUCE

Entomatadas

Makes 18 tacos

2 pounds skirt steak

3 garlic cloves

Salt and pepper to taste

10 tomatoes, coarsely chopped

2 tablespoons olive oil

½ onion, chopped

½ green bell pepper, chopped

½ teaspoon garlic powder

18 corn tortillas, homemade (see page 4) or store-bought

1. Put the steak, garlic, and salt and pepper in a large pot. Add water to cover by 2 to 3 inches and bring to a boil. Reduce the heat and simmer for 30 minutes.

2. Meanwhile, put the tomatoes in a blender and blend until smooth.

3. Heat the oil in a large skillet over medium heat. Add the onion and bell pepper and sauté until the onion is translucent, 3 to 5 minutes. Add the tomato puree and garlic powder, and season with salt and pepper. Reduce the heat to low and simmer for 15 minutes.

4. When the meat is cooked, drain, and discard the garlic. Let the meat cool briefly, then use a fork to shred it.

5. Steam the tortillas (see box on page 143), or dip quickly into a skillet of hot oil to soften them and transfer to paper towels to drain.

6. Fill the center of the tortillas with the meat and roll up. Place seam side down on individual serving plates, top with the warm sauce, and enjoy.

STEAK FAJITAS WITH CITRUS MARINADE

Fajitas are probably one of the most identifiable Mexican dishes served today, undoubtedly because of the manner in which they are presented. At Los Barrios we serve them by the pound in a hot iron skillet that rests on a wooden charger. Everyone's senses totally come alive as the sizzling fajitas fly by. We know that the wonderful aroma that fills the room is certain to coax other diners into ordering their own. Re-create the sizzle at your own backyard barbecue!

Serves 8 to 10

5 pounds beef skirt steak, trimmed of excess fat

Salt and pepper to taste

¼ cup Worcestershire sauce

½ cup salad oil

3 tablespoons lime juice

2 cups water

Put the steak in a glass baking dish large enough for it to lie flat. Combine the remaining ingredients and pour over the steak. Marinate for 1 hour, turning the meat halfway through. Cook on a gas or charcoal grill over medium heat for 20 minutes on each side. Remove from the grill and slice against the grain into julienne strips.

STEAK MILANESA ☀

If you call this "chicken-fried steak, Mexican-style," you take the bite out of its name. But when you call it by its Spanish name, *milanesa*, you can almost taste this mouthwatering delicacy (it's like saying "Pavarotti" before you hear the music), and your senses are ready to indulge in what is coming your way.

Serves 4

1 egg
½ cup milk
1 cup crushed saltines or cornmeal
Four 8-ounce boneless sirloin or round steaks
½ cup vegetable oil
2 lemons, cut in half

1. Beat the egg in a large shallow bowl, then beat in the milk. Spread the cracker crumbs on a plate.

2. Using a meat pounder, pound each steak to flatten and thin it slightly.

3. Heat half the oil in a large skillet over medium heat. Dip the steaks in the egg mixture, then dredge in the crumbs, covering both sides. Add 2 steaks to the hot oil and cook for 5 minutes. Carefully flip the steaks and cook for 5 minutes longer, or to the desired doneness. Set aside. Add remaining oil to the pan and repeat with remaining 2 steaks.

4. Transfer to individual serving plates, squeeze the juice of the lemons over the steaks, and serve immediately.

Serve the steaks with Hot Fried Potatoes (see page 156) and Guacamole (see page 47). You could also serve these with Warm Mild Tomato Sauce (see page 13).

STEAK RANCHERO

Serrano *chiles* vary in heat, but they are usually quite hot. Use the smaller amount for a less spicy dish.

Serves 4

> 2 tablespoons vegetable oil
> 3 tomatoes, sliced
> 1 onion, thinly sliced
> 1 to 2 serrano *chiles* (to taste), sliced
> Four 8-ounce boneless sirloin steaks, thinly sliced
> Salt and pepper to taste

1. Heat the oil in a large skillet over medium heat. Add the tomatoes, onion, and *chiles* and cook until softened, 3 to 4 minutes.

2. Add the meat, season with salt and pepper, and stir well. Cook until the meat is almost cooked, about 7 minutes. Reduce the heat and simmer for 2 minutes longer, to reduce the sauce slightly.

Serve this dish with an Enchilada Verde (see page 119) on the side, along with some rice and Guacamole (see page 47).

STREET VENDOR HAM AND CHEESE SANDWICHES

Tortas de Jamón

Makes 12 open-faced sandwiches

6 *bolillos* (small, elongated hard rolls, available at Latin markets
and some larger supermarkets) or 6-inch French breads

½ cup mayonnaise

1 cup refried beans, homemade (see page 163) or store-bought

12 slices ham, grilled

1 cup shredded Monterey Jack cheese

1 tomato, diced

1 Hass avocado, peeled, pitted, and sliced

Sliced jalapeño *chiles* for garnish (optional)

---

1. Preheat the oven to 325°F.

---

2. Split the *bolillos* in half. Spread the cut sides of the bread with the mayonnaise and top with the beans. Place a slice of ham on each half, and cover with the cheese.

---

3. Arrange the open-faced sandwiches on a cookie sheet and place in the oven for 2 to 3 minutes, until the cheese has melted.

---

4. Top the sandwiches with the tomato, avocado, and *chiles,* if using. Serve hot.

TACOS A LA DIANA ☀

When I was young, my parents owned a very small restaurant, and I loved to go there every day after school. My thing was to go into the kitchen and prepare my own food. I came up with lots of different combinations—some were very good, and others were, well, let's just say that my siblings were not impressed. Tacos a la Diana, however, made it onto the menu at Los Barrios. These are easy to prepare and fun to eat. Even a nine-year-old can make them!

Serves 4

1 cup vegetable oil

12 corn tortillas, homemade (see page 4) or store-bought

1½ cups shredded cooked chicken

1½ cups Guacamole (see page 47)

¾ cup sour cream

1. Heat the oil in a large skillet over medium-high heat until hot. One at a time, dip the tortillas into the hot oil to soften them, just a few seconds. Transfer to paper towels to drain.

2. Put 2 tablespoons of the chicken on each tortilla, top each with a heaping tablespoon of the guacamole, and roll up. Place 3 tacos on each plate and top with the sour cream.

For a lower-calorie alternative to fried tortillas, you can "steam" them in the microwave. One or two at a time, dip the tortillas in water, place on a paper towel, and cover with another paper towel. Microwave for 30 seconds on low, and proceed as directed.

TAMALE PIE

$\mathcal{H}$omemade tamales involve a lot of work and time—which most people don't have. Fortunately for tamale lovers, there are a lot of companies dedicated to making them. They come filled with a variety of ingredients, including beans, chicken, and cheese. This is a great quick-and-easy recipe.

Serves 6 to 8

2½ cups Green Tomatillo Sauce (see page 119)

1¼ cups sour cream

One 15-ounce can creamed corn

1 cup fresh or canned corn kernels

2 dozen prepared pork, chicken, or bean tamales (available
   at larger grocery stores and at Latin markets),
   corn husks removed

2 cups shredded *queso Chihuahua* or Monterey Jack cheese

Sliced roasted poblano *chiles* (see page 79)

1. Preheat the oven to 350°F. Grease a 9 by 13-inch baking dish.

2. Combine the sauce, sour cream, creamed corn, and corn kernels in a bowl and mix well. Arrange half the tamales in the bottom of the prepared pan. Pour the sauce mixture over them. Top with the remaining tamales, and scatter the cheese on top.

3. Cover the pan with foil and bake for 30 to 40 minutes. Garnish with the *chiles*.

TAMALES A LA MEXICANA

The beginning of December marks tamale season in San Antonio. Of course, we have tamales all year round, but come December, they are in high demand for holiday parties. Although they may contain all sorts of fillings, the traditional ones are made with pork, chicken, or beans and jalapeños. By the end of the month, though, we have had our share of tamales for a while, so we freeze whatever we have left. We wait a few weeks, then break them out when we are ready for more. This recipe is a great variation on traditional tamales. Try it and see how wonderful these are!

Serves 6 to 8

> 3 dozen prepared tamales (available at larger grocery stores
>   and at Latin markets), corn husks removed
> 2 cups fresh or canned corn kernels
> 2 cups shredded *queso Chihuahua* or Monterey Jack cheese
> ¼ cup sour cream
> One 7-ounce can green *chiles*
> 2 tablespoons chopped pimientos

1. Preheat the oven to 325°F. Grease a 9 by 13-inch baking dish.

2. Place a layer of tamales in the prepared baking dish. Top with a layer of corn, then cheese, sour cream, and *chiles,* and sprinkle with pimientos. Repeat the process with the remaining ingredients. Bake for 30 minutes, or until bubbly.

Serve these tamales with Refried Beans (see page 163) and Los Barrios Salsa (see page 7).

TAMARIND PORK LOIN

Serves 6 to 8

One 5-pound pork loin roast
Salt and pepper to taste
½ cup soy sauce
½ pound tamarinds
2 tablespoons vegetable oil
¾ cup packed brown sugar

1. Season the pork with salt and pepper. Put it in a baking dish and sprinkle with ¼ cup of the soy sauce. Let marinate for 1 hour.

2. Bring a pot of water to a boil. Cook the tamarinds for 15 minutes. Drain and allow to cool. Peel each tamarind and cut in half to remove the pit. Mash well and set aside.

3. Preheat the oven to 350°F.

4. Heat the oil in a large skillet over medium heat. Add the pork and brown on all sides. Return to the baking dish.

5. Combine the tamarind, the brown sugar, the remaining ¼ cup soy sauce, and salt and pepper, mixing thoroughly. Pour the sauce over the pork, cover, and bake for 2 hours, until cooked.

6. Slice the roast on a cutting board. Arrange the slices in the baking dish, basting them with the pan juices. Return to the oven for an additional 10 minutes.

LOS BARRIOS FAMILY COOKBOOK

VERMICELLI NOODLE SOUP WITH MEATBALLS

Fideos con Albóndigas

This really is a soup that eats like a meal!

Serves 6 to 8

MEATBALLS

1½ pounds ground beef

¼ cup white rice

2 eggs

1 tablespoon all-purpose flour

1 tablespoon salt

¼ teaspoon pepper

VERMICELLI

3 tablespoons vegetable oil

One 12-ounce package vermicelli

½ onion, sliced

½ green bell pepper, sliced

6 serrano *chiles* with stems (see Note)

3 tomatoes, quartered

1 tablespoon salt, plus more to taste

½ teaspoon ground cumin

¼ teaspoon garlic powder

¼ teaspoon pepper

1. To make the meatballs, fill a large pot with 4 quarts of water and bring to a boil.

2. Meanwhile, combine all the meatball ingredients in a bowl, mixing well. Form the mixture into meatballs the size of a golf ball. Add the meatballs to the boiling water, reduce the heat to medium-low, and simmer for 15 minutes.

3. While the meatballs are cooking, heat the oil in a large pot over medium heat. Add the vermicelli and toss back and forth with 2 spoons until golden brown, 5 to 6 minutes; do not allow the noodles to burn. Add the onion, bell pepper, and *chiles* and sauté until the onion is translucent, about 5 minutes.

4. Meanwhile, combine the tomatoes, the 1 tablespoon salt, the cumin, garlic powder, and pepper in a blender. Add 1 cup water from the meatballs and blend until smooth. Add the tomato puree to the vermicelli, stirring well, and simmer for 5 minutes.

5. Add the tomato mixture to the meatballs and their broth and season with salt.

NOTE: Leaving the stems on the *chiles* prevents them from bursting during cooking, which would release their seeds—the source of their heat. To make individual servings spicier, simply serve a *chile* to anyone who wants one, so they can cut open the *chile* and stir the seeds into their soup.

Serve the soup with Refried Beans (see page 163) and warm corn tortillas (see page 4).

SIDE DISHES

Charro-Style Beans 151

Chorizo-Vegetable Casserole 152

Creamy Mashed Potatoes 153

Garden Rice with Shrimp 154

Grilled Corn on the Cob 155

Hot Fried Potatoes 156

Kay's Tortilla and Black Bean Casserole 157

Mexican Rice 159

Nana's Stuffing 160

Oven-Roasted Sweet Potatoes

with Cognac 162

Refried Beans 163

Shrimp and Rice Salad

with Peas and Pimientos 164

Spanish Rice 165

Spicy Pepper Strips in Cream Sauce 166

Sweet Potato Soufflé 167

Traditional Pot of Beans 168

CHARRO-STYLE BEANS

Frijoles a la Charra

Serves 8

1½ pounds dried pinto beans, picked over and rinsed

½ head garlic

1½ tablespoons salt

¼ pound bacon (5 slices), cut into small dice

1 onion, diced

6 serrano *chiles,* chopped

1 tomato, diced

Chopped cilantro for garnish

1. Combine the beans and garlic in a large pot and add water to cover by 2 to 3 inches. Bring to a boil over high heat and boil for 2 hours. After the first hour, check the water level and add a cup or two of warm water if necessary. About 30 minutes before the beans are cooked, add the salt.

2. Meanwhile, lightly brown the bacon in a large skillet over medium heat, 4 to 5 minutes. Add the onion and *chiles* and sauté until the onion is golden brown, 5 to 6 minutes. Stir in the tomato. Remove from the heat.

3. When the beans are tender, stir in the sautéed ingredients and simmer for 10 minutes longer.

4. Serve garnished with cilantro.

CHORIZO-VEGETABLE CASSEROLE

Serves 8 to 10

4 tablespoons (½ stick) butter

½ pound chorizo (Mexican sausage), casings removed, crumbled

3 onions, chopped

2 cups asparagus tips

2 cups canned artichoke hearts

1 cup sliced mushrooms

Salt to taste

3 cups shredded mozzarella cheese

1. Preheat the oven to 350°F.

2. Melt the butter in a large skillet over medium heat. Add the sausage and onions and cook, stirring, for 3 to 4 minutes. Add the asparagus, artichoke hearts, and mushrooms. Add salt to taste. Stir well, and cook for 5 minutes.

3. Transfer the vegetable mixture to a baking dish and sprinkle the cheese over the top. Bake for 5 minutes, or until the cheese has completely melted. Serve with Tortilla Chips (see page 12).

CREAMY MASHED POTATOES

Growing up as the youngest of three children definitely had its pros and cons. While I could get away with a lot, I also had to do a lot. I was the one who had to peel the potatoes for my mother's creamy mashed potatoes. Everyone else had a more important job. And since the potatoes were so delicious, everyone always served themselves plenty—which meant I had to peel a lot of potatoes. When we were young, it was my brother, Louie, who took the prize for the biggest serving. Nowadays, it is a tie among all eight of my mother's grandchildren. Try them, and you'll see what brings us running to the table.

Serves 4

4 Idaho potatoes, peeled and quartered

1 teaspoon salt, plus more to taste

5 tablespoons butter, at room temperature

One 5-ounce can evaporated milk

¼ teaspoon white pepper

1. Place the potatoes in a large pot, cover with water, and add the 1 teaspoon salt. Bring to a boil and boil until tender, 20 to 25 minutes.

2. Drain the potatoes and return them to the pot. Add the butter, milk, and pepper and, using a handheld mixer, mix until smooth. Season with salt if necessary.

GARDEN RICE WITH SHRIMP

For an even easier dish, use frozen carrots and peas and frozen cooked shrimp.

Serves 8 to 10

> ¼ cup vegetable oil
>
> 2 cups white rice
>
> ¼ cup diced onion
>
> 4 garlic cloves, minced
>
> 1 teaspoon lime juice
>
> 2 carrots, peeled and diced
>
> 1 cup peas
>
> 1 chicken bouillon cube
>
> 1¼ teaspoons salt
>
> ¼ teaspoon white pepper
>
> 1 cup shrimp, peeled, deveined, and cooked
>
> Sliced roasted poblano *chiles* (see page 79) for garnish (optional)

1. Heat the oil in a large skillet over medium-high heat. Add the rice and cook, stirring, until coated with oil. Add the onion and cook, stirring frequently, until the onion is translucent, 2 to 3 minutes. Drain off any excess oil.

2. Stir in the garlic and lime juice, then stir in 4 cups warm water and bring to a boil. After 1 minute, add the carrots and peas, stirring well. Stir in the chicken bouillon cube, salt, and pepper. Stir in the shrimp. Cover, reduce the heat, and simmer for 15 minutes, or until the rice is tender and all the water has been absorbed.

3. Serve garnished with poblano *chiles*, if desired.

GRILLED CORN ON THE COB

In Mexico City, you always see street vendors selling corn on the cob accompanied by a variety of toppings. I was first introduced to this simple but delicious treat on a visit there in the early 1980s. Nowadays, vendors of grilled corn are popping up on the street corners of downtown San Antonio. You can also find them at many citywide events and in supermarket parking lots. Everyone eats the sweet grilled corn—from small children who love them simply with butter, to adults who order the authentic *elotes*, covered with mayonnaise and sprinkled with crumbly cheese and cayenne pepper (in Mexico City, they use pure ground *chile* powder). We use Parmesan cheese instead—and my mouth waters just thinking about this treat. Anytime we barbecue, there is always corn on the cob alongside the fajitas and steaks on the grill. My children love their ears with everything on them.

Serves 6

6 ears corn, unhusked
¼ cup mayonnaise
½ cup grated Parmesan cheese
Cayenne pepper to taste

1. Prepare a fire in an outdoor grill.

2. Place the corn (still in the husk) on the grill over medium heat and cook for 1 hour, turning often. The husks will blacken—that's what gives the corn its delicious flavor. Remove and discard the husks.

3. Cover the corn with the mayonnaise, then the cheese, and sprinkle with cayenne pepper. Serve hot.

VARIATION: Try a lemon-pepper spice mixture instead of the cayenne.

HOT FRIED POTATOES ☀

Serves 6

2 cups vegetable oil

3 potatoes, peeled and cut lengthwise into 8 wedges each

Salt to taste

Cayenne pepper to taste

1. Heat the oil in a deep pot over medium-high heat until very hot. Add the potatoes and cook, turning once, until golden brown and tender when pierced with a fork, about 5 minutes.

2. Transfer to a napkin-lined platter, season with salt and cayenne pepper, and serve.

These are the potatoes that we serve at Los Barrios with Steak Milanesa (see page 140). They also go great with eggs, or other meat dishes. Season them with any spice you like.

KAY'S TORTILLA AND BLACK BEAN CASSEROLE

I first tasted my friend Kay's casserole at a Fourth of July party, and I think I almost finished the whole thing myself. If you're having a party, try this recipe—you won't be disappointed.

Serves 6 to 8

2 cups chopped onion

1½ cups chopped green bell pepper

2 garlic cloves, finely chopped

¾ cup Los Barrios Salsa (see page 7) or store-bought

2 teaspoons ground cumin

4 cups drained canned black beans

12 corn tortillas, homemade (see page 4) or store-bought

2 cups shredded *queso Chihuahua* or Monterey Jack cheese

2 cups shredded lettuce

3 tomatoes, chopped

½ cup sour cream

½ cup pitted and sliced black olives

1.   Preheat the oven to 350°F.

2.   Combine the onion, pepper, garlic, salsa, cumin, and beans in a large skillet and bring to a simmer over medium heat. Cook, stirring frequently, for 3 to 4 minutes.

3.   Arrange 6 of the tortillas in the bottom of a 9 by 13-inch baking dish, overlapping them as necessary. Spread half of the bean mixture over the tortillas and sprinkle with half of the cheese. Repeat the layering process with the remaining tortillas, bean mixture, and cheese.

4.   Cover the dish with foil and bake for 30 minutes. Carefully remove the foil (watch out for the steam), and garnish with the lettuce, tomatoes, sour cream, and olives.

This can also be served as a vegetarian meal or with tortilla chips for dipping. If you want to make the dish spicier, add some chopped jalapeños to the garnish.

MEXICAN RICE ☀

The compliments you will receive for this dish will put you on a very high cloud indeed.

Serves 4 to 6

3 tomatoes, coarsely chopped

1 tablespoon Lipton chicken flavor base

1 garlic clove, coarsely chopped

1 teaspoon salt

1 cup water

½ cup vegetable oil

1½ cups white rice

½ green bell pepper, sliced

¼ onion, sliced

1. Combine the tomatoes, chicken base, garlic, and salt in a blender and blend until smooth. Add the water and blend well.

2. Heat the oil in a large skillet over medium heat. Add the rice and cook, stirring, until it begins to brown, 2 to 3 minutes. Add the bell pepper and onion and allow to cook for 2 to 3 more minutes until tender. Drain off any excess oil.

3. Add the tomato mixture to the rice and cook for 2 to 3 minutes. Add 2 cups hot water, stirring well, then cover, reduce the heat, and simmer for 10 minutes. Reduce the heat to low and cook until the rice is tender and all the liquid is absorbed, 5 to 10 minutes longer.

NANA'S STUFFING

This is my mother-in-law's stuffing recipe, and it is out of this world. You can prepare the giblets a day ahead to save time.

Serves 12

3 pounds turkey giblets

1 onion

3 garlic cloves

Salt and pepper to taste

1 pound pork sausage, casings removed, crumbled

3 celery stalks, chopped

1 green or red bell pepper, chopped

One 8-ounce can water chestnuts, drained and chopped

1 cup raisins

1 cup chopped pecans

One 16-ounce package stuffing mix

1 cup beef broth

1. Combine the giblets, onion, and garlic in a large pot and add water to cover by 4 to 6 inches. Season with salt and pepper and bring to a boil. Reduce the heat to a lively simmer and cook until the giblets are tender, $2\frac{1}{2}$ to 3 hours. Drain, and discard the onion and garlic. Let the giblets cool slightly.

2. Preheat the oven to 350°F. Grease a 9 by 13-inch baking dish.

3. Finely chop the giblets; set aside.

4. Brown the sausage in a large skillet over medium heat, stirring often, 6 to 8 minutes. Drain off any excess fat, and transfer the sausage to a large bowl. Add the giblets and all the remaining ingredients, stirring until the stuffing mix is evenly moistened.

5. Place the stuffing in the prepared baking dish. Bake for 35 minutes, or until crunchy on top.

OVEN-ROASTED SWEET POTATOES WITH COGNAC

This tasty side dish can also be served as a dessert.

Serves 4

1 pound sweet potatoes, peeled
4 tablespoons (½ stick) butter
Juice of 3 oranges
½ cup honey
¼ cup Cognac or other brandy
½ to ¾ cup chopped pecans (optional)

1. Place the sweet potatoes in a large pot and add water to cover by 3 inches. Bring to a boil and cook until tender, about 30 minutes. Drain and let cool slightly.

2. Meanwhile, preheat the oven to 350°F. Grease a 9 by 13-inch baking dish.

3. Slice the sweet potatoes and layer them in the prepared baking dish. Dot the top of the potatoes with the butter. Combine the orange juice, honey, and Cognac and pour over them. Bake for 20 minutes.

4. Garnish with the chopped nuts, if desired, and serve immediately.

REFRIED BEANS

Use these great refried beans for bean and cheese tacos, bean and cheese nachos, bean and cheese chalupas, or in a side of rice and beans—life doesn't get any better.

Serves 4 to 6

1 tablespoon vegetable oil or lard

2 cups cooked pinto beans, mashed with a potato masher
or pureed in a blender

1. Heat the oil in a large skillet over medium-high heat until very hot.

2. Add the beans and cook, stirring constantly, for 6 to 8 minutes.

SHRIMP AND RICE SALAD WITH
PEAS AND PIMIENTOS

This dish is very easy to prepare—and wonderful to eat. It's always a crowd pleaser, and it's sure to have your guests asking for more.

Serves 4 to 6

2 cups cooked white rice

1½ cups cooked baby shrimp

1 cup frozen peas, thawed

1 green bell pepper, finely chopped

¼ cup finely chopped pimiento-stuffed olives

2 tablespoons chopped pimientos

1 tablespoon chopped jalapeño *chile*

1 tablespoon finely chopped onion

1 cup mayonnaise

½ teaspoon salt

⅛ teaspoon pepper

Romaine lettuce leaves for serving

12 cherry tomatoes for garnish

1. Combine all the ingredients except the lettuce and tomatoes in a large bowl, mixing well.

2. Mound on a platter lined with lettuce leaves, and garnish with the cherry tomatoes.

VARIATION: Substitute 2 cups cooked pasta (elbow macaroni, penne, fusilli) for the rice.

SPANISH RICE

My mom makes the best rice in the world. Whether it's her Spanish rice or her Garden Rice with Shrimp (see page 154), she just has it down. Many of my friends have asked her to teach them how it is done—or to give them her secret ingredients. There is no secret ingredient, other than a lot of love. We serve this at most of our parties at home, and someone always asks for the recipe.

Serves 6 to 8

¼ pound (1 stick) butter
½ onion, diced
1 green bell pepper, diced
2 cups white rice
2 carrots, peeled and diced
2 chicken bouillon cubes, dissolved in 2 cups hot water

1. Melt the butter in a large skillet over low heat. Add the onion and bell pepper and cook until softened, about 3 minutes. Add the rice and cook, stirring, until coated with butter. Add the carrots and the bouillon broth, then add 4 cups water and bring to a boil. Increase the heat to high and cook, uncovered, for 3 minutes.

2. Reduce the heat to low, cover, and cook until the rice is tender and all the water has been absorbed, about 10 minutes longer.

This rice is the perfect complement to any chicken dish.

SPICY PEPPER STRIPS IN CREAM SAUCE

Rajas Poblano en Crema

This is a traditional Mexican dish. Served in tacos (see pages 23, 24, 132, 138, and 143), or as a side dish on its own, it is a real crowd pleaser.

Serves 4

2 tablespoons vegetable oil

1 garlic clove

1 onion, sliced

6 poblano *chiles*, roasted (see page 79), peeled, seeded, and cut into strips

3½ cups diced mozzarella cheese

2 cups half-and-half

1. Heat the oil in a large saucepan over high heat. Add the garlic and cook until fragrant, 1 to 2 minutes. Remove and discard the garlic, and reduce the heat to medium-high. Add the onion and cook until softened, 2 to 3 minutes. Add the *chiles* and cook for 3 to 4 minutes.

2. Add the cheese, reduce the heat to medium, and stir in the half-and-half. Cook, stirring, until the cheese has melted. Serve immediately.

Serve these with warm flour or corn tortillas (see page 6 or 4).

SWEET POTATO SOUFFLÉ

Soufflé de Camote

I learned this recipe from my mother-in-law, but it took me several attempts to get it right. Not because it is difficult—on the contrary, it is a piece of cake. The problem was that because it's so simple, I would try to do several steps at once, such as adding all the melted butter at the same time rather than dividing it between the filling and the topping. Follow the directions, and you will love the outcome.

Serves 10 to 12

> 2 cups mashed cooked sweet potatoes
>
> 2 eggs, beaten
>
> 1¼ cups sugar
>
> 12 tablespoons (1½ sticks) butter, melted and divided between 2 small bowls
>
> 1 cup milk
>
> ½ teaspoon ground nutmeg
>
> ½ teaspoon ground cinnamon
>
> 1 teaspoon almond extract
>
> ¾ cup crushed cornflakes
>
> ½ cup packed brown sugar
>
> ½ cup chopped pecans

1. Preheat the oven to 400°F. Grease a 9-inch pie plate.

2. Combine the sweet potatoes, eggs, sugar, half of the butter, the milk, nutmeg, cinnamon, and almond extract in a large bowl, mixing well. Pour into the prepared pie plate and bake for 20 to 25 minutes until set.

3. Combine the cornflakes, brown sugar, nuts, and the remaining butter, mixing well. Spread the mixture over the sweet potatoes and bake for another 10 minutes.

TRADITIONAL POT OF BEANS

Frijoles de Olla

This was my father's favorite dish, and it is my brother's favorite as well. If Louie had to choose only one dish for the rest of his life, it would be these beans. These freeze well and are great to have on hand for impromptu parties.

Makes 2 quarts

1 pound dried pinto beans, picked over and rinsed
4 garlic cloves
2½ teaspoons salt

1. Put the beans and garlic in a large pot, add 2 quarts water and the salt, and bring to a boil. Reduce the heat and simmer until tender, 2 to 2½ hours.

2. Discard the garlic cloves and serve the beans as is, or mash them with a potato masher or puree them in a blender until smooth.

DESSERTS

Buñuelos with Apples   171

Caramel-Covered Crepes   172

Dessert Nachos   173

Easy Rice Pudding   174

Flan   175

Frozen Vanilla Milk Pops   177

Lemon-Berry Pie   178

Mango-Cajeta Angel Food Cake   179

Mexican Bread Pudding   180

Old-fashioned Pound Cake   182

Our Favorite Tapioca Pudding   183

Peach-Pecan Upside-Down Cake   184

Tía Marta's Pecan Pie   186

BUÑUELOS WITH APPLES

Buñuelos are a Fiesta favorite as well as a Christmastime staple in our home. They remind me of a sugared doughnut, except that they are flat and crunchy. You can top them with fruit, but they are also great on their own. *Cajeta* is a very rich caramel sauce that can accompany many desserts, especially good on top of ice cream. As a child I remember placing a heaping spoonful on a tortilla, rolling it up, and devouring it—delicious!

Serves 12

8 Granny Smith or Rome apples, peeled, cored, and diced

1 tablespoon sugar

2 cups water

2 cinnamon sticks

12 *buñuelos* (see Note)

1 quart vanilla ice cream

¾ cup *cajeta* or caramel sauce (see Note)

2 tablespoons Bailey's Irish Cream (optional)

1. Combine the apples and sugar in a bowl, tossing to mix. Set aside.

2. Combine the water and cinnamon sticks in a medium saucepan and bring to a boil. Boil until the liquid has reduced to ½ cup, about 15 minutes. Strain the syrup, and stir it into the apple mixture.

3. Place 1 *buñuelo* on each dessert plate and top with a scoop of ice cream. Spoon the apple mixture, with its syrup, over the ice cream, and drizzle with the *cajeta*. Drizzle the liqueur over the top of each, if desired, and serve immediately.

N O T E : *Buñuelos* and *cajeta* can be found at Latin markets and some larger supermarkets.

CARAMEL-COVERED CREPES

Packaged crepes are available in the refrigerator section of larger super-markets. *Cajeta* can be found at Latin markets and some larger supermarkets.

Serves 5

> 2½ cups *cajeta* or caramel sauce
>
> One 4.5-ounce package 7-inch crepes (10 crepes)
>
> 1 cup chopped pecans

---

1. Heat the *cajeta* in the microwave or in a saucepan over low heat.

---

2. Prepare the crepes as directed on the package. Spread ¼ cup of *cajeta* over each crepe, roll up, and place seam side down on a serving platter. Top with more *cajeta* and the nuts (see Note).

NOTE: If you have any leftover *cajeta*, it is wonderful over ice cream.

DESSERT NACHOS

These sweet nachos are always a hit. Just about any combination of fruit works well. In San Antonio, we have several *buñuelo* factories that supply us with bite-sized *buñuelos*; they can be found at Latin markets and some larger supermarkets.

Makes 2 dozen mini nachos

2 pints strawberries, hulled and chopped

4 to 6 kiwis, peeled and chopped

1 pint raspberries

1 pint blueberries

24 mini *buñuelos*

Chocolate sauce for drizzling

1. Combine the fruit in a large bowl, stirring gently to mix well.

2. Place the *buñuelos* on a serving platter. Spoon the fruit over the *buñuelos*, drizzle chocolate sauce over the top, and serve.

EASY RICE PUDDING

Arroz con Leche

Serves 10

1 cup white rice

1 cinnamon stick

One 12-ounce can evaporated milk

½ cup raisins (optional)

½ cup sugar

Ground cinnamon for sprinkling

1. Bring 5 cups water to a boil in a large saucepan. Add the rice and cinnamon stick and cook for 15 to 20 minutes. Add the milk, and raisins if desired, stirring well, then stir in the sugar. Turn the heat down to low and cook, covered, about 5 minutes longer, until rice is soft. Remove from the heat and let cool. Discard cinnamon stick.

2. Transfer the rice pudding to a serving bowl. Serve warm, or cover and refrigerate until chilled. Just before serving, sprinkle cinnamon over the top

VARIATION: To jazz up the pudding, you can add ¼ cup Kahlúa or amaretto when you add the milk. Other garnish choices include nuts and fresh fruit.

FLAN ☀

Flan, a silky-smooth custard with a sweet caramel topping, is one of the most traditional of Mexican desserts.

Serves 12 to 14

CUSTARD

One 14-ounce can sweetened condensed milk

One 12-ounce can evaporated milk

4 ounces cream cheese, at room temperature

7 eggs

1 teaspoon vanilla extract

CARAMEL

2 cups sugar

---

1. Preheat the oven to 325°F. Have a 9-inch round glass pie plate ready.

---

2. To make the custard, combine all the ingredients in a blender and blend until smooth. Set aside.

---

3. To make the caramel, put the sugar in a large deep pot and cook over low heat, stirring gently with a wooden spoon, until the sugar has melted and turned golden brown. Quickly but carefully pour the caramel into the pie plate. It will harden immediately.

---

4. Pour the custard mixture over the caramel. Put the pie plate into a larger baking pan and add ½ inch boiling water to the larger pan. Bake for 2 hours, or until firm. Let cool.

---

5. When the flan is cool, run a knife around the edges of the dish to release it, and invert onto a large rimmed serving platter. Refrigerate for 2 hours, or until chilled.

---

6. To serve, cut the flan into wedges and place on dessert plates, drizzling some of the caramel over each slice.

FROZEN VANILLA MILK POPS

How do you keep yourself cool in the hot Texas sun? Try the treat we enjoyed as children. I remember feeling so grown up the first time I made this, thinking to myself what a good cook I was!

Serves 4

> One 12-ounce can evaporated milk
> 2 tablespoons sugar
> 2 teaspoons vanilla extract

1. Combine all the ingredients in a blender and blend for 30 seconds. Pour the mixture into ice cube trays. Cover with plastic wrap, and stick a toothpick through the plastic into each cube, to serve as a handle.

2. Freeze until firm, at least 6 hours, or overnight. Remove the cubes from the trays and enjoy.

VARIATION: Add ⅛ teaspoon ground cinnamon to the evaporated milk mixture.

LEMON-BERRY PIE

Serves 6 to 8

One 12-ounce can evaporated milk

One 14-ounce can sweetened condensed milk

1¼ cups fresh lemon juice

One 9-inch prepared graham cracker crust

1 cup sliced strawberries or whole blueberries or raspberries

1. Combine the evaporated milk, condensed milk, and lemon juice in a large bowl, mixing well.

2. Pour into the piecrust and top with the berries. Refrigerate for 4 to 6 hours, or overnight. Serve chilled.

MANGO-CAJETA ANGEL FOOD CAKE

When you bite into this dessert, you will think you have gone to heaven. The recipe is very easy, and it's delicious, too. Angel food cake will never be the same again!

Serves 10 to 12

¾ cup milk

2 cups *cajeta* (see Note) or caramel sauce

¼ cup sweetened condensed milk

½ cup chopped walnuts

1 prepared angel food cake

2 cups diced mango

1. Bring the milk to a boil in a large saucepan. Add the *cajeta,* condensed milk, and walnuts, stirring until well mixed. Remove from the heat.

2. Slice the angel food cake and place on dessert plates. Spoon the sauce over the cake, and top with the mangoes.

NOTE: *Cajeta* is available at Latin markets and some larger supermarkets.

VARIATION: Blueberries or raspberries can be substituted for the mangoes.

MEXICAN BREAD PUDDING

Capirotada

In Mexico, this dessert is prepared every Friday during the Lenten season. Everyone I know makes her own version—I love trying different *capirotada* recipes, because they are all so varied.

Serves 12

AGUA DE PILONCILLO

2½ *piloncillos* (see Note)

1 cinnamon stick

1½ teaspoons ground anise

2 quarts water

CAPIROTADA

4 tablespoons (½ stick) butter

1 loaf French bread, cut into ½-inch slices

1 cup raisins

1 cup coarsely chopped pecans

1 cup slivered almonds

2 cups grated *queso Chihuahua* or Monterey Jack cheese

---

1. Preheat the oven to 325°F. Grease a 9 by 13-inch baking dish.

---

2. To make the *agua de piloncillo*, combine all the ingredients in a large saucepan and bring to a boil, stirring to dissolve the sugar. Remove from the heat. Discard the cinnamon stick.

---

3. To make the *capirotada*, butter one side of each slice of bread and arrange buttered-side up on a cookie sheet. Bake for 5 to 6 minutes, until golden on top. Turn the bread over and bake for 4 to 5 minutes longer, until toasted on the second side. Remove from the oven.

---

4. Line the bottom of the prepared baking dish with a single layer of bread. Top with half the raisins, pecans, almonds, and cheese. Ladle some of the syrup over the top. Create an additional layer with the remaining ingredients, pouring all the remaining syrup over the top.

5. Cover the pudding with foil and bake for 30 minutes, or until the liquid has been absorbed.

NOTE: *Piloncillos* are small brown cones of unrefined sugar. They are available at Latin markets and some larger supermarkets.

OLD-FASHIONED POUND CAKE

This was one of my father's favorites. My mother always baked it for him to enjoy with his coffee.

Serves 12

3/4 pound (3 sticks) butter, at room temperature

One 16-ounce box confectioners' sugar

6 eggs

1 tablespoon vanilla extract

1 teaspoon lemon juice

4 cups cake flour

1. Preheat the oven to 325°F. Grease a Bundt pan.

2. In a large bowl, cream the butter and sugar together. Beat in the eggs, one at a time. Beat in vanilla and lemon juice. Add flour and mix until well blended. Pour the batter into the prepared pan and smooth the top.

3. Bake for 1 hour and 45 minutes, or until a toothpick inserted in the center comes out clean. Set the pan on a wire rack to cool. Turn cake out after 10 or 15 minutes.

VARIATION: Add 1 cup raisins, tossed with about 1 tablespoon of the cake flour, to the batter (flouring them prevents them from falling to the bottom of the cake as it bakes).

OUR FAVORITE TAPIOCA PUDDING

This is a great dessert to follow a light lunch.

Serves 6

One 12-ounce can evaporated milk

¾ cup sugar

3 tablespoons tapioca

¾ cup water

2 egg yolks

Pinch of salt

1 teaspoon vanilla extract

Sliced peaches for garnish (optional)

1. Combine the milk and sugar in a large saucepan and heat over medium heat for 1 to 2 minutes; be careful not to let the milk boil.

2. Meanwhile, combine the tapioca and water in a medium bowl. Beat in the egg yolks. Stir in the salt.

3. Gradually add the egg mixture to the warm milk mixture, stirring constantly. Stir in the vanilla. Cook, stirring, until the mixture comes just to a simmer; do not let it boil, or it may curdle. Pour into a 9-inch pie plate or small baking dish and let cool slightly, then refrigerate until chilled, at least 2 hours.

4. Just before serving, garnish the pudding with sliced peaches or other fresh fruit, if desired.

PEACH-PECAN UPSIDE-DOWN CAKE

Pastel de Durazno

Serves 12

CAKE

2 cups Bisquick mix

2 eggs

1 cup sugar

1 cup milk

¾ cup vegetable oil

2 teaspoons vanilla extract

TOPPING

¼ pound (1 stick) butter, melted

1 cup packed brown sugar

One 15¼-ounce can sliced peaches, drained

About ½ cup pecan halves

1. Preheat the oven to 375°F.

2. To make the cake batter, combine all the ingredients in a large bowl, whisking together until blended. Set aside.

3. To make the topping, pour the melted butter into a Bundt pan. Sprinkle the brown sugar evenly over the butter. Arrange the peaches on top. Place a pecan half between each peach slice.

4. Carefully pour the batter over the peaches. Bake for 40 minutes, or until a toothpick inserted in the center of the cake comes out clean. Transfer the pan to a wire rack to cool for 10 minutes, then invert.

5. Serve the cake warm, with ice cream, if desired.

VARIATION: Substitute one peeled, cored, and thinly sliced Granny Smith apple for the peaches.

TÍA MARTA'S PECAN PIE

Serves 8

One 14-ounce can sweetened condensed milk

¾ cup water

¼ cup unsweetened cocoa powder

3 eggs

1 teaspoon vanilla extract

1 cup chopped pecans

One 9-inch prepared graham cracker crust

---

1. Preheat the oven to 325°F.

---

2. Combine the milk, water, cocoa, eggs, and vanilla in a blender and blend well. Transfer to a bowl and stir in the pecans. Pour the mixture into the piecrust.

---

3. Bake for 50 minutes, or until set. Transfer to a wire rack to cool.

Serve the pie with _cajeta_ *(available at Latin markets and some larger supermarkets) or caramel sauce drizzled on top.*

BEVERAGES

Agua de Horchata   189

Limonada Fresca   190

Margarita's Margarita   191

Mexican Coffee   192

Mexican Hot Chocolate   193

Red Fruit Punch   194

Refreshing Watermelon Delight   195

Sangría   196

AGUA DE HORCHATA

If you have ever traveled to Mexico, you may have seen street vendors selling flavored "waters." This recipe is for a popular milky-looking rice drink. It is very tasty, and it is also considered a cure-all for children with upset tummies. Plan ahead; you need to soak the rice for 24 hours.

Makes 1 gallon

1 pound white rice
2 cinnamon sticks
One 14-ounce can sweetened condensed milk

1. Combine the rice and cinnamon sticks in a large bowl and add water to cover. Cover and refrigerate for 24 hours.

2. Remove and discard cinnamon sticks. In batches, transfer the rice and soaking liquid to a blender and blend until smooth. Using a fine sieve, strain the liquid into a bowl, pressing on the solids with a wooden spoon to squeeze out all the liquid; discard the solids.

3. Stir the milk into the rice water. Cover and refrigerate until chilled, before serving.

LIMONADA FRESCA ☀

There is nothing quite like the taste of this delicious fresh limeade. It is refreshing and thirst-quenching. Serve it in a glass pitcher, garnished with lime slices.

Makes 1 gallon

4 cups sugar, or more to taste

1 gallon water

1 cup fresh lime juice, or more to taste

1 lime, cut into thin slices

1. Combine the sugar and water in a large pitcher, stirring to dissolve the sugar. Stir in the lime juice. Taste, and add more sugar or lime juice if necessary.

2. Add the lime slices to the pitcher, and serve the limeade over ice.

MARGARITA'S MARGARITA

Serve these at your next party, and you will be known as the party host of all party hosts. Multiply the recipe as necessary—everyone will want to be added to your guest list!

Serves 1

1½ ounces Cuervo 1800 tequila

1 ounce Grand Marnier

Splash of whiskey sour mix

1 lime wedge

---

1. Pour the tequila and Grand Marnier into a shaker. Add the sour mix, and squeeze the juice of the lime into the shaker. Add ice, and shake to mix.

---

2. Pour into a salt-rimmed margarita glass, and enjoy!

MEXICAN COFFEE

"**W**ow!" "This is great!" "Can you share the recipe with me?" These are the comments you will hear when you serve this coffee. I recently served it at an open house, and people who don't even like coffee were asking for seconds. It's a great combination of flavors, and it goes well with many desserts.

Serves 10 to 12

Hot coffee to serve 10 to 12, brewed with 2 cinnamon sticks
  added to the pot
½ cup packed brown sugar
2 tablespoons chocolate syrup
2 ounces Kahlúa
1 tablespoon Tía Maria (coffee-flavored liqueur)

1. Strain the hot coffee into a heatproof pitcher.

2. Add the remaining ingredients, stir to dissolve the sugar, and serve immediately.

MEXICAN HOT CHOCOLATE

exican hot chocolate is like no other. Made with Mexican chocolate, it has the most wonderful flavor. It is especially good with *pan dulce* or my mom's Old-fashioned Pound Cake (see page 182).

Serves 3 or 4

> 3 cups milk
>
> 1 cinnamon stick
>
> ½ tablet Mexican chocolate (such as Nestlé Abuelita or
> Ibarra brand), broken into pieces
>
> Sugar to taste (optional)

1. Combine the milk and cinnamon stick in a medium saucepan and heat over medium heat until the milk is hot but not boiling. Add the chocolate and stir until melted.

2. Remove and discard the cinnamon stick, and sweeten with sugar, if desired.

RED FRUIT PUNCH

One of my favorite drinks as a child was this great punch, which my aunt would make for birthday parties. All of the children in attendance would be sporting red mustaches as they raced around the backyard from one activity to another!

Makes 4 gallons

4 envelopes unsweetened Tropical Punch Kool-Aid

4 cups sugar

4 cups pineapple juice

1 cup fresh lemon juice

3¼ gallons (13 quarts) water

1. Combine all the ingredients in a large drink cooler or a punch bowl, stirring to dissolve the Kool-Aid and sugar.

2. Add ice, and enjoy.

VARIATION: You can garnish the punch with fresh fruit or with drained canned fruit cocktail.

REFRESHING WATERMELON DELIGHT

Refresco de Sandía

This fruit-flavored water, or *aguas frescas*, is especially delicious, and it looks beautiful served in a clear glass pitcher.

Makes 1 gallon

2 pounds watermelon
3½ quarts water
2 cups sugar

---

1. Remove the seeds from the watermelon, slice the flesh from the rind, and cut it into chunks. Transfer to a blender, in batches if necessary, and blend for a few seconds; there should still be some small chunks of watermelon.

---

2. Combine the water and sugar in a large pitcher, stirring to dissolve the sugar. Stir in the watermelon puree, blending thoroughly. Refrigerate until chilled before serving.

VARIATION: You can substitute cantaloupe for the watermelon.

SANGRÍA ✷

Sangría is a cool, refreshing drink for a summer fiesta. But it's so tasty, it's easy to forget it is made with wine—be careful not to drink too much!

Makes 1½ gallons

2 quarts red wine

2 cups lemon-lime soda

2 cups orange juice

1¼ cups lime juice

2 cups sugar

2 cups applesauce

1 orange, thinly sliced, each slice cut in half

1 lime, thinly sliced, each slice cut in half

1 Red Delicious apple, peeled, cored, and sliced into thin rounds

1. Combine the red wine, soda, orange juice, lime juice, sugar, and applesauce in a large pitcher, stirring to dissolve the sugar. Add the orange, lime, and apple. Refrigerate until chilled.

2. Serve in tall glasses, making sure to include some fruit in each serving.

INDEX

A

Acapulco-Style Ceviche, 31–32
Agua de Horchata, 189
Agua de Piloncillo, 180–81
almonds, in Mexican Bread
    Pudding, 180–81
American cheese:
    Best Tex-Mex Enchiladas, 93
    Breakfast Chilaquiles, 17
    Chalupas Mariachi, 100
    Chalupas Vallarta, 102
    Nachos a la Butler, 51
    Seven-Layer Mexican Bean
        Dip, 52
ancho *chile(s)*, xx
    Sauce, Potato Tacos with,
        24–25
Angel Food Cake, Mango-Cajeta,
    179
appetizers, 29–56
    Avocado Cocktail, 33
    Avocado Mini Tapas, 34
    Avocado Spread, Spicy, 54
    Beef or Chicken Empanadas,
        36–37
    Ceviche, Acapulco-Style,
        31–32
    Ceviche Cocktail, 38
    Chalupas, Summer, 55
    Cheese, Flaming, 46
    Chicharrón de Queso, 39
    Chile con Queso (Warm
        Jalapeño Cheese Dip), 40
    Chipotle Dip, Creamy, 44

Cilantro Dip, 41
Fiesta Dip, 45
Guacamole, 47
Ham and Cheese Stacks, 48
Jicama Ceviche, 49
Nachos a la Butler, 51
Queso, Mama's, 50
Seven-Layer Mexican Bean
    Dip, 52
Shrimp Quesadillas, 136–37
Sour Cream Nachos, 53
Texas Caviar, 56
Tortilla and Black Bean
    Casserole, Kay's, 157–58
Veggies, Beachfront, 35
apple(s):
    Buñuelos with, 171
    Pecan Upside-Down Cake,
        185
    San Antonio Chicken Salad,
        85
    Sangría, 196
Apricot Ribs, Jammin', 125
Arroz con Leche, 174
Arroz con Pollo (Chicken with
    Rice), 89
artichoke hearts:
    Chorizo-Vegetable Casserole,
        152
    San Antonio Chicken Salad,
        85
asadero, in Mama's Queso, 50
Asado de Puerco, 131

asparagus, in Chorizo-Vegetable
    Casserole, 152
avocado(s), xx
    Chalupas Mariachi, 100
    Chalupas Mexicanas, 101
    Cocktail, 33
    and Corn Salad with
        Green-Gold Dressing,
        77
    Cuernavaca Salad with
        Honey-Mustard
        Vinaigrette, 78
    Louie's Salad, 82
    Mini Tapas, 34
    Spread, Spicy, 54
    Texas Caviar, 56
    Tortilla Soup, 71–72
    see also Guacamole

B

bananas:
    Hearty Fruit-and-Nut
        Oatmeal, 18
    Nature's Breakfast, 22
Beachfront Veggies, 35
bean(s):
    Black, and Tortilla Casserole,
        Kay's, 157–58
    black, in Texas Caviar, 56
    Black, Mayonnaise, 116
    Charro-Style, 151
    Dip, Seven-Layer Mexican,
        52

bean(s) *(cont'd)*
  garbanzo, in Hot and Spicy
    Tlalpeño Soup, 64–65
  kidney, in San Antonio
    Chicken Salad, 85
  Soup, Creamy, 61
  Tamale Pie, 144
  Tamales a la Mexicana, 145
  Traditional Pot of, 168
Beans, Refried, 163
  Chalupas Mariachi, 100
  Chalupas Mexicanas, 101
  Chalupas Vallarta, 102
  Nachos a la Butler, 51
  Seven-Layer Mexican Bean
    Dip, 52
  Sour Cream Nachos, 53
  Summer Chalupas, 55
beef:
  Burgers with Herbs,
    Roland's, 135
  Chiles Rellenos, 113–14
  Chili con Carne, 115
  Empanadas, 36–37
  Fiesta Dip, 45
  Flank Steak with Cheese and
    Tomatillo Sauce, 123
  Meatballs, Spicy Tomato Soup
    with Cilantro and, 69–70
  Meatballs, Vermicelli Noodle
    Soup with, 147–48
  Menudo (Tripe Soup), 67–68
  Nachos a la Butler, 51
  Picadillo, 129
  Ribs, Jammin' Apricot, 125
  Steak Fajitas with Citrus
    Marinade, 139
  Steak Milanesa, 140
  Steak Ranchero, 141
  Steak Sandwich, Commerce
    Street, 116–17

Stew *(Carne Guisada)*, 96
Stew Zuazua-Style, 90–91
Tacos, Soft Rolled, with
  Tomato Sauce, 138
and Vegetable Soup, Hearty,
  62–63
berry(ies):
  Lemon Pie, 178
  see also specific berries
beverages, 187–96
  Agua de Horchata, 189
  Coffee, Mexican, 192
  Hot Chocolate, Mexican, 193
  Limonada Fresca, 190
  Margarita, Margarita's, 191
  Red Fruit Punch, 194
  Sangría, 196
  Watermelon Delight, Re-
    freshing, 195
Biscuits, Sassy, 26
black bean(s):
  Mayonnaise, 116
  Texas Caviar, 56
  and Tortilla Casserole, Kay's,
    157–58
blueberry(ies):
  Cajeta Angel Food Cake, 179
  Dessert Nachos, 173
  Lemon-Berry Pie, 178
Bread Pudding, Mexican,
  180–81
breakfast, 15–27
  Biscuits, Sassy, 26
  Chilaquiles, 17
  Eggs, Mexican-Style, 21
  Fruit-and-Nut Oatmeal,
    Hearty, 18
  Hash Browns, Spicy, 27
  Mama's, 19
  Nature's, 22
  Potato and Egg Tacos, 23

  Potato Tacos with Ancho
    Chile Sauce, 24–25
  Sausage (Mexican) and Eggs,
    20
buñuelos:
  with Apples, 171
  Dessert Nachos, 173
Burgers with Herbs, Roland's,
  135
buttermilk, in Sassy Biscuits, 26
Butternut Squash Soup, 59

C
cabbage:
  Hearty Beef and Vegetable
    Soup, 62–63
  Spicy Jell-O Vegetable Salad,
    86
  Summer Chalupas, 55
Cabrito en Salsa, 126–27
Cactus with Eggs and Chile
  Sauce, 94–95
cajeta:
  Buñuelos with Apples, 171
  Caramel-Covered Crepes, 172
  Mango Angel Food Cake, 179
cakes:
  Angel Food, Mango-Cajeta,
    179
  Peach-Pecan Upside-Down,
    184–85
  Pound, Old-Fashioned, 182
Caldo de Pollo, 66
Caldo de Res, 62–63
Caldo Tlalpeño, 64–65
Camarones al Ajillo, 124
cantaloupe:
  Delight, Refreshing, 195
  Los Valles Fruit Cup, 81
Capirotada, 180–81
caramel:

Buñuelos with Apples, 171
-Covered Crepes, 172
Flan, 175–76
Mango-Cajeta Angel Food
    Cake, 179
Carne Guisada (Beef Stew),
    96
carrots:
    Beachfront Veggies, 35
    Garden Rice with Shrimp, 154
    Hearty Beef and Vegetable
        Soup, 62–63
cascarones, 42
    Colorful, 43
casero style, xv
casseroles:
    Breakfast Chilaquiles, 17
    Chilaquiles with Chicken, 112
    Chorizo-Vegetable, 152
    Tamale Pie, 144
    Tamales a la Mexicana, 145
    Tortilla and Black Bean,
        Kay's, 157–58
Caviar, Texas, 56
Cazuela de Pollo con Aceitunas,
    109–10
celebrations, 42
    Colorful Cascarones for, 43
ceviche:
    Acapulco-Style, 31–32
    Cocktail, 38
    Jicama, 49
chalupa(s), 97
    Especiales, 99
    Mariachi, 100
    Mexicanas, 101
    "Sandwiches" with Sour
        Cream, 98
    Summer, 55
    Vallarta, 102
Chalupas con Crema, 98

Charro-Style Beans, 151
Cheddar cheese:
    Enchiladas with Spinach,
        121–22
    Nachos a la Butler, 51
    Sassy Biscuits, 26
cheese, xx
    Chicharrón de Queso, 39
    Flaming, 46
    Flank Steak with Tomatillo
        Sauce and, 123
    and Ham Sandwiches, Street
        Vendor, 142
    and Ham Stacks, 48
    Jalapeño Dip, Warm (*Chile
        con Queso*), 40
    Mama's Queso, 50
    Sour Cream Nachos, 53
    see also American cheese; feta
        cheese; Monterey Jack
        cheese; mozzarella cheese;
        *queso añejo; queso Chi-
        huahua;* Velveeta cheese
Chicharrón de Queso, 39
chicken(s):
    breasts, skinless, boneless,
        xxi
    Breasts in Creamy Poblano
        Sauce, 105
    Chalupa "Sandwiches" with
        Sour Cream, 98
    Chalupas Especiales, 99
    Chalupas Vallarta, 102
    Chilaquiles with, 112
    Chipotle, 106
    in Cilantro Sauce, 107
    Empanadas, 36–37
    Enchiladas Rancheras, 118
    Enchiladas Verdes, 119–20
    Enchiladas with Spinach,
        121–22

    fryer, xx
    Hot and Spicy Tlalpeño-Style
        Soup, 64–65
    Louie's Salad, 82
    Make-Me-Crazy Grill
        Marinade for, 8
    with Olives, 109–10
    with Rice (*Arroz con Pollo*),
        89
    Rice Soup, Mama Viola's, 66
    Salad, San Antonio, 85
    Summer Chalupas, 55
    with Summer Squash, 111
    Tacos a la Diana, 143
    Tamale Pie, 144
    Tamales a la Mexicana, 145
    in Tangy Tomato Sauce, 108
    Tortilla Soup, 71–72
    a la Viola, 103–4
chickpeas, see garbanzo beans
chilaquiles:
    Breakfast, 17
    with Chicken, 112
chile(s), xx
    Ancho, Sauce, Potato Tacos
        with, 24–25
    Chipotle, Chicken, 106
    Chipotle, Dip, Creamy, 44
    jalapeño, in Sour Cream
        Nachos, 53
    poblano, in Spicy Pepper
        Strips in Cream Sauce, 166
    poblano, roasting, 79
    Poblano, Sauce, Creamy,
        Chicken Breasts in, 105
    con Queso (Warm Jalapeño
        Cheese Dip), 40
    Red, Sauce, Pork Tips in, 131
    Rellenos, 113–14
    Salsa, Los Barrios, 7
    Texas Caviar, 56

chili:
    con Carne, 115
    powder, in Enchilada Gravy
        Sauce, 3
chipotle:
    Chicken, 106
    Dip, Creamy, 44
Chips, Tortilla, 12
    Breakfast Chilaquiles, 17
    Nachos a la Butler, 51
    Sour Cream Nachos, 53
chocolate:
    Hot, Mexican, 193
    Mexican Coffee, 192
    sauce, in Dessert Nachos,
        173
chorizo (Mexican sausage):
    Chalupas Mexicanas, 101
    and Eggs, 20
    Flaming Cheese, 46
    Sassy Biscuits, 26
    Vegetable Casserole, 152
Chorizo con Huevos, 20
cilantro:
    Dip, 41
    Mousse, 41
    Sauce, Chicken in, 107
    Spicy Tomato Soup with
        Meatballs and, 69–70
citrus:
    Grill Marinade, Make-Me-
        Crazy, 8
    Marinade, Steak Fajitas with,
        139
cod:
    Acapulco-Style Ceviche,
        31–32
    Ceviche Cocktail, 38
Coffee, Mexican, 192
Cognac, Oven-Roasted Sweet
    Potatoes with, 162

Commerce Street Steak
    Sandwich, 116–17
corn:
    and Avocado Salad with
        Green-Gold Dressing, 77
    on the Cob, Grilled, 155
    Hearty Beef and Vegetable
        Soup, 62-63
    masa mix, xx
    Tamale Pie, 144
    Tamales a la Mexicana, 145
    Texas Caviar, 56
corn tortilla(s), xx
    and Black Bean Casserole,
        Kay's, 157–58
    Chilaquiles with Chicken, 112
    Chips, 12
    chips, in Breakfast Chi-
        laquiles, 17
    chips, in Nachos a la Butler,
        51
    chips, in Sour Cream Nachos,
        53
    Enchiladas, Best Tex-Mex, 93
    Enchiladas Rancheras, 118
    Enchiladas Verdes, 119–20
    Enchiladas with Spinach,
        121–22
    Ham and Cheese Stacks, 48
    Homemade, 4–5
    Potato Tacos with Ancho
        Chile Sauce, 24–25
    Shrimp Quesadillas, 136–37
    Soft Rolled Beef Tacos with
        Tomato Sauce, 138
    Soup, 71–72
    "steaming" in microwave, 143
    store-bought, heating, xxi
    Tacos a la Diana, 143
    see also chalupa(s)
Cortadillo Zuazua, 90–91

Costillas con Mermelada, 125
cranberries, dried:
    Hearty Fruit-and-Nut
        Oatmeal, 18
    Nature's Breakfast, 22
cream cheese, xxi
    Cilantro Dip, 41
    Spicy Avocado Spread, 54
Crepes, Caramel-Covered, 172
cucumbers, in Beachfront
    Veggies, 35
Cuernavaca Salad with Honey-
    Mustard Vinaigrette, 78
custard (Flan), 175–76

D

desserts, 169–86
    Bread Pudding, Mexican,
        180–81
    Buñuelos with Apples, 171
    Caramel-Covered Crepes, 172
    Flan, 175–76
    Frozen Vanilla Milk Pops, 177
    Fruit Cup, Los Valles, 81
    Lemon-Berry Pie, 178
    Mango-Cajeta Angel Food
        Cake, 179
    Nachos, 173
    Peach-Pecan Upside-Down
        Cake, 184–85
    Pecan Pie, Tía Marta's, 186
    Pound Cake, Old-Fashioned,
        182
    Rice Pudding, Easy, 174
    Sugar Tortillas, 11
    Sweet Potatoes, Oven-
        Roasted, with Cognac, 162
    Tapioca Pudding, Our
        Favorite, 183
dips:
    Avocado Cocktail, 33

Chipotle, Creamy, 44
Cilantro, 41
Fiesta, 45
Green Tomatillo Sauce,
    119–20
Guacamole, 47
Jalapeño Cheese, Warm (*Chile
    con Queso*), 40
Pico de Gallo, 9
Salsa, Los Barrios, 7
Salsa Ranchera, 10
Seven-Layer Mexican Bean, 52
Texas Caviar, 56
Tortilla and Black Bean
    Casserole, Kay's, 157–58
Tortilla Chips for, 12

E

egg(s), xxi
    Breakfast Chilaquiles, 17
    Cactus with Chile Sauce and,
        94–95
    Mama's Breakfast, 19
    Mexican Sausage and, 20
    Mexican-Style, 21
    and Potato Tacos, 23
eggshells:
    cascarones, 42
    Cascarones, Colorful,
        43
Empanadas, Beef or Chicken,
    36–37
enchilada(s), 92–93
    Best Tex-Mex, 93
    Gravy Sauce, 3
    Rancheras, 118
    with Spinach, 121–22
    Verdes, 119–20
Ensalada Blanca, 82
Entomatadas, 138
entrées, 87–148

Beef Stew (*Carne Guisada*),
    96
Beef Stew Zuazua-Style,
    90–91
Beef Tacos, Soft Rolled, with
    Tomato Sauce, 138
Burgers with Herbs,
    Roland's, 135
Cactus with Eggs and Chile
    Sauce, 94–95
Chalupa "Sandwiches" with
    Sour Cream, 98
Chalupas Especiales, 99
Chalupas Mariachi, 100
Chalupas Mexicanas, 101
Chalupas Vallarta, 102
Chicken a la Viola, 103–4
Chicken Breasts in Creamy
    Poblano Sauce, 105
Chicken Chipotle, 106
Chicken in Cilantro Sauce,
    107
Chicken in Tangy Tomato
    Sauce, 108
Chicken Salad, San Antonio,
    85
Chicken with Olives, 109–10
Chicken with Rice (*Arroz con
    Pollo*), 89
Chicken with Summer
    Squash, 111
Chilaquiles with Chicken, 112
Chiles Rellenos, 113–14
Chili con Carne, 115
Enchiladas, Best Tex-Mex, 93
Enchiladas Rancheras, 118
Enchiladas Verdes, 119–20
Enchiladas with Spinach,
    121–22
Flank Steak with Cheese and
    Tomatillo Sauce, 123

Goat, Milk-Fed, in Tomato
    Sauce, 126–27
Ham and Cheese Sandwiches,
    Street Vendor, 142
Louie's Salad, 82
Oxtails, 128
Picadillo, 129
Pork Chop Lover's Delight,
    130
Pork Loin, Tamarind, 146
Pork Tips in Red *Chile* Sauce,
    131
Red Snapper in Garlic-Butter
    Sauce, 134
Ribs, Jammin' Apricot, 125
Shrimp, Garlic, 124
Shrimp Quesadillas, 136–37
Steak Fajitas with Citrus
    Marinade, 139
Steak Milanesa, 140
Steak Ranchero, 141
Steak Sandwich, Commerce
    Street, 116–17
Tacos, Puffy, 132–33
Tacos a la Diana, 143
Tamale Pie, 144
Tamales a la Mexicana, 145
Tortilla and Black Bean
    Casserole, Kay's, 157–58
Vermicelli Noodle Soup with
    Meatballs, 147–48

F

Fajitas, Steak, with Citrus
    Marinade, 139
feta cheese:
    Chalupas Especiales, 99
    Enchiladas Rancheras, 118
    Fresh Tomato Salad, 80
    San Antonio Chicken Salad,
        85

feta cheese (*cont'd*)

Summer Chalupas, 55

Tortilla Soup, 71–72

Fideo, 72

Fideos con Albóndigas,

147–48

Fiesta Dip, 45

fish:

Ceviche, Acapulco-Style,

31–32

Ceviche Cocktail, 38

Make-Me-Crazy Grill

Marinade for, 8

Red Snapper in Garlic-Butter

Sauce, 134

see also shrimp

Flaming Cheese, 46

Flan, 175–76

Flank Steak with Cheese and

Tomatillo Sauce, 123

Flay, Bobby, 42, 132

flour, xx

flour tortillas, xx

Chicharrón de Queso, 39

Homemade, 6

Mexican Sausage and Eggs,

20

Potato and Egg Tacos, 23

"steaming" in microwave,

143

store-bought, heating, xxi

Sugar Tortillas, 11

Frijoles a la Charra, 151

Frijoles de Olla, 168

Frozen Vanilla Milk Pops, 177

fruit:

Cup, Los Valles, 81

-and-Nut Oatmeal, Hearty,

18

Red, Punch, 194

see also specific fruits

G

garbanzo beans (chickpeas):

Hot and Spicy Tlalpeño-Style

Soup, 64–65

Texas Caviar, 56

Garden Rice with Shrimp,

154

garlic, xx, xxi

Butter Sauce, Red Snapper in,

134

powder, xx

Shrimp, 124

Goat, Milk-Fed, in Tomato

Sauce, 126–27

Grand Marnier, in Margarita's

Margarita, 191

granola:

Hearty Fruit-and-Nut

Oatmeal, 18

Nature's Breakfast, 22

Green-Gold Dressing, 77

Green Tomatillo Sauce,

119–20

grill(ed):

Burgers with Herbs,

Roland's, 135

Corn on the Cob, 155

Marinade, Make-Me-Crazy,

8

Steak Fajitas with Citrus

Marinade, 139

Guacamole, 47

Chalupa "Sandwiches" with

Sour Cream, 98

Chalupas Especiales,

99

Chalupas Vallarta, 102

Nachos a la Butler, 51

Seven-Layer Mexican Bean

Dip, 52

Tacos a la Diana, 143

H

ham:

and Cheese Sandwiches,

Street Vendor, 142

and Cheese Stacks, 48

Harding, Deborah, xviii

Hash Browns, Spicy, 27

Hearty Beef and Vegetable Soup,

62–63

Hearty Fruit-and-Nut Oatmeal,

18

herbs, xxi

hominy, in *Menudo* (Tripe

Soup), 67–68

Honey-Mustard Vinaigrette, 78

Hot and Spicy Tlalpeño-Style

Soup, 64–65

Hot Chocolate, Mexican, 193

Huevos a la Mexicana, 21

I

ice cream, in Buñuelos with

Apples, 171

ingredients:

to have on hand, xx

helpful hints for, xxi

J

jalapeño chile(s), xx

Cheese Dip, Warm (*Chile con*

Queso), 40

Sour Cream Nachos, 53

Jammin' Apricot Ribs, 125

Jell-O:

Mango Salad, 83

Vegetable Salad, Spicy, 86

jicama:

Beachfront Veggies, 35

Ceviche, 49

Pico de Gallo, 9

Texas Caviar, 56

K

Kahlúa, in Mexican Coffee, 192
Kay's Tortilla and Black Bean
    Casserole, 157–58
kidney beans, in San Antonio
    Chicken Salad, 85
kiwis, in Dessert Nachos, 173
Kool-Aid, in Red Fruit Punch,
    194

L

Lagasse, Emeril, vii, 42
lemon:
    Berry Pie, 178
    Red Fruit Punch, 194
lime:
    Limonada Fresca, 190
    Sangría, 196
Limonada Fresca, 190
Los Barrios Restaurant, xiii–xix
    origins of, xiii–xiv
    Louie's Salad, 82

M

Make-Me-Crazy Grill Marinade,
    8
Mama's Breakfast, 19
Mama's Queso, 50
Mama Viola's Chicken Rice
    Soup, 66
Manchego cheese, in *Chicharrón
    de Queso*, 39
mango(es):
    -Cajeta Angel Food Cake, 179
    Los Valles Fruit Cup, 81
    Pico de Gallo, 9
    Salad, 83
Margarita, Margarita's, 191
Marinade, Grill, Make-Me-
    Crazy, 8
masa mix, corn, xx

Mashed Potatoes, Creamy, 153
Mayonnaise, Black Bean, 116
meatballs:
    Spicy Tomato Soup with
        Cilantro and, 69–70
    Vermicelli Noodle Soup with,
        147–48
Menudo (Tripe Soup), 67–68
Mexican:
    Bean Dip, Seven-Layer, 52
    Bread Pudding, 180–81
    Coffee, 192
    Hot Chocolate, 193
    Rice, 159
    sausage, *see* chorizo
Mexican-Style Eggs, 21
Milk Pops, Vanilla, Frozen, 177
molcajete, xxi
Monterey Jack cheese, xx
    Chilaquiles with Chicken, 112
    Cuernavaca Salad with
        Honey-Mustard Vinai-
        grette, 78
    Enchiladas Verdes, 119–20
    Enchiladas with Spinach,
        121–22
    Flaming Cheese, 46
    Ham and Cheese Sandwiches,
        Street Vendor, 142
    Ham and Cheese Stacks, 48
    Louie's Salad, 82
    Mama's Queso, 50
    Mexican Bread Pudding,
        180–81
    San Antonio Chicken Salad,
        85
    Seven-Layer Mexican Bean
        Dip, 52
    Shrimp Quesadillas, 136–37
    Spicy Hash Browns, 27
    Tamale Pie, 144

Tamales a la Mexicana, 145
Tortilla and Black Bean
    Casserole, Kay's, 157–58
mortars and pestles, xxi
Mousse, Cilantro, 41
mozzarella cheese:
    Chorizo-Vegetable Casserole,
        152
    Spicy Pepper Strips in Cream
        Sauce, 166
mushrooms, in Chorizo-
    Vegetable Casserole, 152
Mustard-Honey Vinaigrette, 78
"must haves," 1–13
    Corn Tortillas, Homemade,
        4–5
    Enchilada Gravy Sauce, 3
    Flour Tortillas, Homemade, 6
    Grill Marinade, Make-Me-
        Crazy, 8
    Pico de Gallo, 9
    Salsa, Los Barrios, 7
    Salsa Ranchera, 10
    Sugar Tortillas, 11
    Tomato Sauce, Warm Mild, 13
    Tortilla Chips, 12

N

nachos:
    a la Butler, 51
    Dessert, 173
    Sour Cream, 53
Nachos Agrios, 53
Nana's Stuffing, 160–61
Nature's Breakfast, 22
Nopalitos, 94–95
nut(s), xxi
    Fruit-and-, Oatmeal, Hearty,
        18
    toasting, 60
    see also specific nuts

O

oatmeal:
  Fruit-and-Nut, Hearty, 18
  Nature's Breakfast, 22
oil, vegetable, xxi
Old-Fashioned Pound Cake, 182
Olives, Chicken with, 109–10
onions, xx, xxi
  Chorizo-Vegetable Casse-
    role, 152
  Hearty Beef and Vegetable
    Soup, 62–63
orange, in Sangría, 196
orange roughy, in Acapulco-
  Style Ceviche, 31–32
Oxtails, 128

P

pans, xxi
Papas Rancheras, 27
pasta:
  and Shrimp Salad with Peas
    and Pimientos, 164
  Vermicelli Noodle Soup with
    Meatballs, 147–48
  Vermicelli Tomato Soup, 73
Pastel de Durazno, 184–85
Peach-Pecan Upside-Down
  Cake, 184–85
peas:
  Garden Rice with Shrimp,
    154
  Shrimp and Rice Salad with
    Pimientos and, 164
pecan(s):
  Caramel-Covered Crepes,
    172
  Flour Tortillas with, Home-
    made, 6

Hearty Fruit-and-Nut
  Oatmeal, 18
Mexican Bread Pudding,
  180–81
Nature's Breakfast, 22
Peach Upside-Down,
  184–85
Pie, Tía Marta's, 186
pepper (black), xx
pepper(s) (bell), xx
  Hearty Beef and Vegetable
    Soup, 62–63
  Red, Green, and Yellow,
    Salad, 84
  roasting, 79
  Sassy Biscuits, 26
  Spicy Jell-O Vegetable Salad,
    86
pepper(s) *(chile)*:
  Strips in Cream Sauce,
    Spicy, 166
  see also chile(s)
Picadillo, 129
  Beef Empanadas, 36
Pico de Gallo, 9
pies:
  Lemon-Berry, 178
  Pecan, Tía Marta's, 186
  Tamale, 144
pimientos:
  Shrimp and Rice Salad with
    Peas and, 164
  Sour Cream Nachos, 53
pineapple:
  Los Valles Fruit Cup, 81
  Red Fruit Punch, 194
pinto beans:
  Charro-Style, 151
  Chili con Carne, 115
  Creamy Bean Soup, 61

Refried Beans, 163
  Traditional Pot of Beans, 168
poblano *chile(s)*:
  roasting, 79
  Sauce, Creamy, Chicken
    Breasts in, 105
  Spicy Pepper Strips in
    Cream Sauce, 166
Pollo al Cilantro, 107
Pollo con Calabacita, 111
Pollo en Salsa, 108
pork:
  Chop Lover's Delight, 130
  Loin, Tamarind, 146
  sausage, in Nana's Stuffing,
    160–61
  Tamale Pie, 144
  Tamales a la Mexicana, 145
  Tips in Red Chile Sauce, 131
  see also chorizo; ham
potato(es):
  and Egg Tacos, 23
  Hash Browns, Spicy, 27
  Hearty Beef and Vegetable
    Soup, 62–63
  Hot Fried, 156
  Mashed, Creamy, 153
  Tacos with Ancho Chile
    Sauce, 24–25
pots, xxi
Pound Cake, Old-Fashioned,
  182
provolone cheese, in Sour
  Cream Nachos, 53
puddings:
  Bread, Mexican, 180–81
  Rice, Easy, 174
  Tapioca, Our Favorite, 183
Puffy Tacos, 132–33
Punch, Red Fruit, 194

Q

Quesadillas, Shrimp, 136–37
queso añejo:
    Chalupas Especiales, 99
    Chalupas Mexicanas, 101
    San Antonio Chicken Salad, 85
    Summer Chalupas, 55
    Tortilla Soup, 71–72
queso Chihuahua, xx
    Chilaquiles with Chicken, 112
    Cuernavaca Salad with
        Honey-Mustard
        Vinaigrette, 78
    Enchiladas Verdes, 119–20
    Enchiladas with Spinach,
        121–22
    Flaming Cheese, 46
    Ham and Cheese Stacks, 48
    Louie's Salad, 82
    Mama's Queso, 50
    Mexican Bread Pudding,
        180–81
    San Antonio Chicken Salad,
        85
    Seven-Layer Mexican Bean
        Dip, 52
    Shrimp Quesadillas, 136–37
    Spicy Hash Browns, 27
    Tamale Pie, 144
    Tamales a la Mexicana, 145
    Tortilla and Black Bean
        Casserole, Kay's, 157–58
Queso Flameado, 46
queso fresco:
    Enchiladas Rancheras, 118
    Fresh Tomato Salad, 80

R

raisins, in Mexican Bread
    Pudding, 180–81

Rajas Poblano en Crema, 166
ranchero(a)(s):
    Enchiladas, 118
    Salsa, 10
    Steak, 141
raspberry(ies):
    Cajeta Angel Food Cake, 179
    Dessert Nachos, 173
Red, Green, and Yellow Pepper
    Salad, 84
Red Chile Sauce, Pork Tips in,
    131
Red Fruit Punch, 194
red snapper:
    Ceviche Cocktail, 38
    in Garlic-Butter Sauce, 134
Refresco de Sandía, 195
refried beans, see Beans,
    Refried
Ribs, Jammin' Apricot, 125
rice:
    Agua de Horchata, 189
    Chicken Soup, Mama Viola's,
        66
    Chicken with (*Arroz con Pollo*),
        89
    Garden, with Shrimp, 154
    Mexican, 159
    Pudding, Easy, 174
    and Shrimp Salad with Peas
        and Pimientos, 164
    Spanish, 165
    Spanish, in Hearty Beef and
        Vegetable Soup, 62–63
roasting:
    peppers, 79
    poblano *chiles,* 79
Rodríguez, Francisco D. (Paco),
    xiii–xv
Roland's Burgers with Herbs, 135

S

Sábanas de Res, 123
salad dressings:
    Green-Gold, 77
    Honey-Mustard Vinaigrette,
        78
salads, 75–86
    Chicken, San Antonio, 85
    Corn and Avocado, with
        Green-Gold Dressing, 77
    Cuernavaca, with Honey-
        Mustard Vinaigrette, 78
    Jell-O Vegetable, Spicy,
        86
    Los Valles Fruit Cup, 81
    Louie's, 82
    Mango, 83
    Red, Green, and Yellow
        Pepper, 84
    Shrimp and Rice, with Peas
        and Pimientos, 164
    Tomato, Fresh, 80
salsa:
    Los Barrios, 7
    Pico de Gallo, 9
    Ranchera, 10
    Texas Caviar, 56
Salsa Dulce de Tomate, 13
salt, xx
San Antonio Chicken Salad,
    85
sandwiches:
    Ham and Cheese, Street
        Vendor, 142
    Steak, Commerce Street,
        116–17
    "Sandwiches," Chalupa, with
        Sour Cream, 98
Sangría, 196
Sassy Biscuits, 26

sauces:
  Black Bean Mayonnaise, 116
  Enchilada Gravy, 3
  Green Tomatillo, 119–20
  Spinach, 121–22
  Tomato, Warm Mild, 13
sausage:
  Mexican, see chorizo
  Nana's Stuffing, 160–61
seafood, see fish; shrimp
seasonings, xx
Selena, xvi
serrano chiles, xx
Seven-Layer Mexican Bean Dip,
  52
shortening, xx
shrimp:
  Enchiladas with Spinach, 122
  Garden Rice with, 154
  Garlic, 124
  Make-Me-Crazy Grill
    Marinade for, 8
  Quesadillas, 136–37
  and Rice Salad with Peas and
    Pimientos, 164
side dishes, 149–68
  Beans, Charro-Style, 151
  Beans, Refried, 163
  Beans, Traditional Pot of, 168
  Chorizo-Vegetable Casserole,
    152
  Corn and Avocado Salad with
    Green-Gold Dressing, 77
  Corn on the Cob, Grilled, 155
  Cuernavaca Salad with
    Honey-Mustard
    Vinaigrette, 78
  Jell-O Vegetable Salad, Spicy,
    86
  Mango Salad, 83

Pepper Strips in Cream
  Sauce, Spicy, 166
Potatoes, Creamy Mashed,
  153
Potatoes, Hot Fried, 156
Red, Green, and Yellow
  Pepper Salad, 84
Rice, Mexican, 159
Rice, Spanish, 165
Rice with Shrimp, Garden,
  154
Shrimp and Rice Salad with
  Peas and Pimientos, 164
Stuffing, Nana's, 160–61
Sweet Potatoes, Oven-
  Roasted, with Cognac, 162
Sweet Potato Soufflé, 167
Tomato Salad, Fresh, 80
Tortilla and Black Bean
  Casserole, Kay's, 157–58
Sincronizadas de Jamón, 38
Sopa de Albóndigas con Cilantro,
  69–70
Sopa de Frijol, 61
Soufflé, Sweet Potato, 167
Soufflé de Camote, 167
soups, 57–73
  Bean, Creamy, 61
  Beef and Vegetable, Hearty,
    62–63
  Butternut Squash, 59
  Chicken Rice, Mama Viola's,
    66
  Hot and Spicy Tlalpeño-
    Style, 64–65
  Oxtail, 128
  Tomato, Spicy, with Meatballs
    and Cilantro, 69–70
  Tortilla, 71–72
  Tripe (*Menudo*), 67–68

Vermicelli Noodle, with
  Meatballs, 147–48
Vermicelli Tomato, 73
sour cream, xxi
  Cilantro Dip, 41
  Creamy Chipotle Dip, 44
  Nachos, 53
  Spicy Avocado Spread, 54
Spanish Rice, 165
spices, xxi
spicy:
  Avocado Spread, 54
  Hash Browns, 27
  and Hot Tlalpeño-Style Soup,
    64–65
  Jell-O Vegetable Salad, 86
  Pepper Strips in Cream
    Sauce, 166
  Tomato Soup with Meatballs
    and Cilantro, 69–70
Spinach, Enchiladas with,
  121–22
spreads:
  Spicy Avocado, 54
  see also dips
squash:
  Butternut, Soup, 59
  Summer, Chicken with,
    111
steak:
  Fajitas with Citrus Marinade,
    139
  Flank, with Cheese and
    Tomatillo Sauce, 123
  Milanesa, 140
  Ranchero, 141
  Sandwich, Commerce Street,
    116–17
stews:
  Beef (*Carne Guisada*), 96

Beef, Zuazua-Style,
90–91
Chili con Carne, 115
strawberries:
Dessert Nachos, 173
Lemon-Berry Pie, 178
Los Valles Fruit Cup, 81
Nature's Breakfast, 22
Street Vendor Ham and Cheese
Sandwiches, 142
Stuffing, Nana's, 160–61
sugar:
Piloncillo, Agua de, 180–81
Tortillas, 11
Summer Chalupas, 55
sweet potato(es):
Oven-Roasted, with Cognac,
162
Soufflé, 167
Swiss cheese, in Sour Cream
Nachos, 53

T
tacos:
Beef, Soft Rolled, with
Tomato Sauce, 138
a la Diana, 143
Potato, with Ancho Chile
Sauce, 24–25
Potato and Egg, 23
Puffy, 132–33
*Tacos de Papa con Chile
Colorado,* 24–25
Tacos de Papa con Huevos,
23
tamale(s):
a la Mexicana, 145
Pie, 144
Tamarind Pork Loin, 146
Tapas, Avocado Mini, 34

Tapioca Pudding, Our Favorite,
183
tatuma squash, in Chicken with
Summer Squash, 111
tequila, xxi
Margarita, Margarita's, 191
Texas Caviar, 56
Tía Maria, in Mexican Coffee,
192
Tía Marta's Pecan Pie, 186
Tlalpeño-Style Soup, Hot and
Spicy, 64–65
Tomatillo Sauce, Green, 119–20
tomato(es), xx
Cuernavaca Salad with
Honey-Mustard
Vinaigrette, 78
Fresh, Salad, 80
Hearty Beef and Vegetable
Soup, 62–63
Mama's Breakfast, 19
Mexican Rice, 159
Pico de Gallo, 9
Salsa, Los Barrios, 7
Salsa Ranchera, 10
Sauce, Milk-Fed Goat in,
126–27
Sauce, Tangy, Chicken in, 108
Sauce, Warm Mild, 13
Soup, Spicy, with Meatballs
and Cilantro, 69–70
Texas Caviar, 56
Vermicelli Soup, 73
Tortas de Jamón, 142
tortilla(s), xx
"steaming" in microwave, 143
store-bought, heating, xxi
see also corn tortilla(s); flour
tortillas
Tortillas de Azúcar, 11

Tostadas (Tortilla Chips), 12
Traditional Pot of Beans, 168
Treviño, Robert, xvi
Tripe Soup *(Menudo),* 67–68
Tropical Punch Kool-Aid, in Red
Fruit Punch, 194
turkey, Nana's Stuffing for,
160–61

U
Upside-Down Cake, Peach-
Pecan, 184–85

V
Vanilla Milk Pops, Frozen,
177
vegetable(s):
Beachfront Veggies, 35
and Beef Soup, Hearty,
62–63
Chorizo Casserole, 152
Jell-O Salad, Spicy, 86
quick-cooking, xxi
vegetable oil, xxi
Velveeta cheese:
Breakfast Chilaquiles, 17
Chile con Queso (Warm
Jalapeño Cheese Dip), 40
Creamy Chipotle Dip, 44
Fiesta Dip, 45
vermicelli (noodle):
Soup with Meatballs, 147–48
Tomato Soup, 73
Vinaigrette, Honey-Mustard,
78

W
walnuts, in Hearty Fruit-and-
Nut Oatmeal, 18
Warm Mild Tomato Sauce, 13

watermelon:
    Delight, Refreshing, 195
    Los Valles Fruit Cup, 81
waters, flavored:
    Agua de Horchata, 189
    Watermelon Delight,
        Refreshing, 195

wine, in Sangría, 196

Y

yogurt, in Nature's Breakfast, 22

Z

Zuazua-Style Beef Stew, 90–91

zucchini:
    Chicken with Summer
        Squash, 111
    Hearty Beef and Vegetable
        Soup, 62–63

DIANA BARRIOS TREVIÑO and her brother, Louie Barrios, own and operate Los Barrios restaurant, which *The New York Times* recently praised as one of the top restaurants in the San Antonio area (although locals have known that for years). She regularly champions Tex-Mex cooking on the *Today* show, and has appeared on *Good Morning America* and *Food Nation with Bobby Flay.*